Better Homes and Gardens®

Hot & Spicy Cooking

First Edition. Second Printing, 1984.
Library of Congress Catalog Card Number: 83 63306
ISBN: 0-696-01422-X (hard cover)
ISBN: 0-696-01420-3 (trade paperback)

BETTER HOMES AND GARDENS® BOOKS
Editor: Gerald M. Knox
Art Director: Ernest Shelton
Managing Editor: David A. Kirchner

Food and Nutrition Editor: Nancy Byal
Department Head, Cook Books: Sharyl Heiken
Associate Department Heads: Sandra Granseth,
    Rosemary C. Hutchinson, Elizabeth Woolever
Senior Food Editors: Julie Henderson, Julia Malloy,
    Marcia Stanley
Associate Food Editors: Jill Burmeister, Molly Culbertson,
    Linda Foley, Linda Henry, Lynn Hoppe, Mary Jo Plutt,
    Maureen Powers, Joyce Trollope
Recipe Development Editor: Marion Viall
Test Kitchen Director: Sharon Stilwell
Test Kitchen Home Economists: Jean Brekke, Kay Cargill,
    Marilyn Cornelius, Maryellyn Krantz, Lynelle Munn,
    Dianna Nolin, Marge Steenson, Cynthia Volcko

Associate Art Directors: Linda Ford Vermie, Neoma Alt West,
    Randall Yontz
Copy and Production Editors: Marsha Jahns,
    Mary Helen Schiltz, Carl Voss, David A. Walsh
Assistant Art Directors: Harijs Priekulis, Tom Wegner
Senior Graphic Designers: Alisann Dixon, Lynda Haupert,
    Lyne Neymeyer
Graphic Designers: Mike Burns, Mike Eagleton, Deb Miner,
    Stan Sams, D. Greg Thompson, Darla Whipple,
    Paul Zimmerman

Vice President, Editorial Director: Doris Eby
Executive Director, Editorial Services: Duane L. Gregg

General Manager: Fred Stines
Director of Publishing: Robert B. Nelson
Vice President, Retail Marketing: Jamie Martin
Vice President, Direct Marketing: Arthur Heydendael

HOT AND SPICY COOKING
Editor: Jill Burmeister
Copy and Production Editor: Carl Voss
Graphic Designer: Lynda Haupert
Electronic Text Processor: Donna Russell

Contributing Photographers: Mike Dieter, Scott Little

Our seal assures you that every recipe in *Hot and Spicy Cooking* has been tested in the Better Homes and Gardens® Test Kitchen. This means that each recipe is practical and reliable, and meets our high standards of taste appeal.

On the cover: *Texas Chili* (see recipe, page 16), *TNT Chili* (see recipe, page 18), *and Midwestern Butter Bean Chili* (see recipe, page 19).

Contents

Horseradish root

Poblano pepper
(fresh; mild)

Cayenne peppers
(dried; hot)

Coriander seed

Yellow chili peppers
(fresh; hot)

Serrano peppers
(fresh; hot)

Pasilla pepper
(dried; mildly hot)

Ground
red pepper

Cascabel
peppers
(dried; mildly hot)

Fresh gingerroot

Whole nutmeg

Stick cinnamon

Cardamom seed

Sweet red peppers
(fresh; mild)

California peppers
(dried; mild)

Jalapeño peppers
(fresh; hot)

Chipotle peppers
(dried; very hot)

Mulato peppers
(dried; mild)

Anaheim peppers
(fresh; mild)

Pequin peppers
(dried; hot)

Guajillo pepper
(dried; hot)

What makes food hot and spicy? The answer lies in many of the chili peppers and spices you see here. Keep in mind that more is not necessarily better; flavor should never be sacrificed for hotness. And just as vital as how much seasoning you add is how you add it. This book will help you learn to cook herbs, spices, and chili peppers *into* your dishes to achieve a harmony of flavors that labels you a good cook.

Ancho pepper
(dried; mild)

Star anise

Black mustard seed

Crushed red pepper

Szechuan peppercorns

Bay leaves

Chili Peppers

Though chilies do not belong to the pepper family, people started calling them chili peppers in the days of Christopher Columbus and the name has stuck ever since.

A common fallacy is that seeds are the hottest part of a pepper. The heat is actually in the membrane to which the seeds are attached and the ribs that run the length of the inside. For a milder flavor, remove membranes and seeds.

Handling Chili Peppers
Because chili peppers contain volatile oils that can burn skin and eyes, avoid direct contact with the peppers as much as possible. Wear plastic or rubber gloves or work under cold running water. If your bare hands touch the chili peppers, wash your hands and nails well with soap and water.

Preparing Dried Chili Peppers
Rinse dried chili peppers in cold water. Cut them open and discard stems and seeds. Cut the peppers into small pieces with a knife or scissors, as shown below. To soften peppers for use in a sauce, soak them in boiling water for 45 to 60 minutes or till pliable; drain.

Preparing Fresh Chili Peppers
It is often best to peel the firm skin from fresh peppers before using. To loosen the skin for easier peeling, place peppers on a broiler pan 4 inches from heat, as shown below. Broil, turning often, till charred on all sides. Place broiled peppers in a paper or plastic bag. Close bag tightly. Let stand 10 minutes. This steams the peppers so the skin easily peels away from the flesh.

Cut stems from peppers. To remove seeds and ribs, slit open peppers and place seed side up on a flat surface. Use a knife to scrape seeds and ribs from the flesh, as shown below. Slice or chop the peppers as directed in the recipe.

Storing Chili Peppers

Dried chili peppers will keep in a cool, dry place for up to a year. For longer storage, freeze them in an airtight container.

Store fresh peppers in paper bags in the refrigerator for up to 1 week. To freeze, roast peppers; cool and freeze in a plastic bag. The skins will peel off easily as the peppers thaw.

Using Canned Chili Peppers

Rinse both plain and pickled canned chili peppers before using to remove the salty liquid in which they are packed.

To remove the seeds from whole chili peppers, slit them open and use a knife to scrape out the seeds and ribs, as you would do for fresh chili peppers. Chop or slice the chili peppers as directed in the recipe.

Herbs and Spices

The rule of thumb for interchanging fresh and dried herbs is to use three times as much fresh as you would dried. Though ground ginger cannot match the flavor of fresh gingerroot, in a pinch you can substitute about one-fourth of the amount of ground ginger for grated gingerroot.

Grating Fresh Gingerroot

Peel fresh gingerroot, if desired, then grate, as shown below. A 1-inch piece that is ¾ inch in diameter yields about 2 teaspoons grated gingerroot. To store, freeze whole gingerroot in moisture- and vaporproof wrap. You do not need to thaw before grating.

Crushing Dried Herbs and Spices

To release their flavor, crush dried herbs and aromatic seeds with a mortar and pestle, as shown below. Another way to crush herbs is to place them in the palm of one hand and crush them with the thumb of your other hand.

Unforgettable Chicken Wings

Sausage-Stuffed Mushrooms *(see recipe, page 12)*

Avocado-Chicken Dip *(see recipe, page 15)*

(EXTRA HOT) Unforgettable Chicken Wings

12 chicken wings (2 pounds) Cooking oil *or* shortening for deep-fat frying	● Cut off and discard tips of chicken wings. Cut wings at joints to form 24 pieces. Fry wing pieces, a few at a time, in deep hot cooking oil or shortening (375°) for 8 to 10 minutes or till golden brown. Drain on paper towels. Transfer wings to a serving dish.	**All bottled hot pepper sauces are not equal! These wings are "extra hot" when you use the Tabasco brand, but they'll burn less and have more red chili pepper flavor when you use the other hot pepper sauces on the market. Either way you try these fiery wings, you'll never forget the experience.**
3 tablespoons butter *or* margarine 1 2-ounce bottle (¼ cup) bottled hot pepper sauce	● In a saucepan melt butter or margarine. Stir in hot pepper sauce. Pour over wings. Turn wings to coat.	
½ cup dairy sour cream ¼ cup mayonnaise *or* salad dressing 1 tablespoon lime juice Celery sticks (optional)	● For dipping sauce, in a bowl stir together sour cream, mayonnaise or salad dressing, and lime juice. Serve wings with dipping sauce and, if desired, celery sticks. Makes 24.	

Oven-Crisp Tortilla Chips
(see tip, page 15)

Hot Pepper Jelly

Samosas *(see recipe, page 11)*

Hot Pepper Jelly

2 fresh jalapeño *or* serrano peppers, seeded and coarsely chopped (⅓ cup) 1 large green pepper, coarsely chopped (1 cup)	● See instructions on page 6 for handling chili peppers. Using the coarse blade of a food grinder, grind green pepper and jalapeño or serrano peppers. (Or, finely chop green pepper and chili peppers using a food processor or knife.)	This emerald green jelly has the flavor of green peppers with a mild jalapeño zip. If you think you'd like a hotter jelly, substitute serrano peppers for the jalapeños.
6½ cups sugar 1½ cups cider vinegar	● In a 4½-quart Dutch oven combine green pepper mixture, sugar, and vinegar. Bring to boiling; reduce heat. Cover and boil gently, stirring frequently, about 15 minutes or till green pepper mixture becomes transparent.	Savor the jelly with cream cheese on crackers or bagels. Try it as a condiment with beef, lamb, or pork. It also makes a great gift for the hot-and-spicy-food lover.
½ of a 6-ounce package (1 foil pouch) liquid fruit pectin Several drops green food coloring	● Stir in pectin and food coloring. Return to a full rolling boil; boil hard, uncovered, for 1 minute, stirring constantly. Remove from heat. Quickly skim off any foam with a metal spoon. Pour at once into hot sterilized half-pint jars; seal, using metal lids or paraffin. Makes 6 half-pints.	

Garlic and Parmesan Popcorn

3 tablespoons butter *or* margarine ½ teaspoon dried basil, crushed ½ teaspoon garlic powder ½ teaspoon ground red pepper	● In a small saucepan melt butter or margarine over medium-high heat. Stir in dried basil, garlic powder, and ground red pepper. Remove from heat.	**Tired of ho-hum buttered popcorn? Jazz it up by adding a few spices to the butter and tossing in some Parmesan cheese.**
6 cups popped popcorn ¼ cup grated Parmesan cheese	● Pour butter mixture over popcorn; toss to mix well. Add Parmesan cheese; toss again. Makes 6 cups.	

Toasty Snack Mix

¼ cup butter *or* margarine 1 tablespoon bottled hot pepper sauce 1 teaspoon Worcestershire sauce ½ teaspoon garlic salt 2 cups unsalted peanuts	● In a large skillet or wok melt butter or margarine over medium heat. Stir in hot pepper sauce, Worcestershire sauce, and garlic salt. Add peanuts; cook over medium heat about 6 minutes or till lightly browned, stirring constantly.	**In less than 10 minutes, you could be munching this lively nibble mix. Just stir it together in a large skillet (or use a wok if you have one).**
2 cups thin pretzel sticks 2 cups round toasted oat cereal	● Add pretzel sticks and cereal; toss to coat well. Continue cooking over medium heat about 1 minute or till slightly toasted, stirring constantly. Transfer to a bowl. Makes 6 cups.	

Samosas

Also pictured on page 9.

¼ cup chopped onion 2 tablespoons butter *or* margarine 1 teaspoon grated gingerroot ½ teaspoon ground coriander ¼ teaspoon ground red pepper	● In a skillet over medium heat cook chopped onion in 2 tablespoons butter or margarine till onion is tender but not brown. Stir in grated gingerroot, ground coriander, and ground red pepper. Cook and stir 2 minutes more.
1 medium potato, cooked, peeled, and chopped ½ cup cooked peas 2 teaspoons lime juice 1 teaspoon Homemade Garam Masala (see recipe, page 92) *or* garam masala ½ teaspoon salt	● Stir in the chopped cooked potato, cooked peas, lime juice, Homemade Garam Masala or garam masala, and ½ teaspoon salt. Reduce heat to low. Cook 5 minutes more, stirring once or twice.
2 cups all-purpose flour 1 teaspoon salt 2 tablespoons butter *or* margarine ¾ cup plain yogurt	● Combine flour and 1 teaspoon salt. Cut in 2 tablespoons butter till mixture resembles coarse crumbs. Stir in yogurt, mixing with your hands to form a ball. Divide dough into 12 balls. On a floured surface roll each ball into a 5-inch circle. Cut each circle in half. Place a rounded teaspoonful of filling on one side of each half-circle. Brush edges of dough with water. Fold dough over filling. Seal edges with tines of a fork.
Cooking oil *or* shortening for deep-fat frying	● Fry a few at a time in deep hot cooking oil or shortening (375°) for 1 to 2 minutes or till golden. Drain on paper towels. Serve warm. Makes 24.

Samosas, the traditional snack of India, are like little fried pies and can contain any vegetable or meat combination. This version has a rather spicy vegetable filling enclosed in a yogurt pastry. If you like, set out a small bowl of sweet chutney to use for dipping.

Sausage-Stuffed Mushrooms

Pictured on page 8.

18 fresh large mushrooms (about 1 pound)	● Wash mushrooms gently in cold water; pat dry. Remove stems, reserving caps. Finely chop the stems; set aside.
2 tablespoons butter *or* margarine 1 tablespoon dry sherry	● In a 10-inch skillet melt butter or margarine. Add 1 tablespoon dry sherry and the mushroom caps; cook on medium heat for 2 to 3 minutes or till mushrooms caps are slightly golden. Remove with a slotted spoon; drain on paper towels.
¼ pound bulk Italian sausage 2 tablespoons finely chopped onion 1 clove garlic, minced	● Add sausage, onion, and garlic to the skillet. Cook about 5 minutes or till sausage is brown and onion is tender. Add the reserved stems and cook 2 minutes more. Remove from heat; drain.
¼ cup fine dry bread crumbs ¼ cup grated Parmesan cheese 1 tablespoon dry sherry Sliced pimiento	● Mix in bread crumbs, *2 tablespoons* of the Parmesan cheese, and 1 tablespoon dry sherry. Place a rounded tablespoon of the sausage mixture in each cap. Arrange the stuffed mushroom caps in a 12x7½x2-inch baking dish. Bake in a 350° oven for 10 to 15 minutes or till hot. Sprinkle with the remaining Parmesan cheese. Garnish with sliced pimiento. Makes 18.

Italian sausage spices up the stuffing for these mushrooms. Keep in mind that Italian sausage can vary in seasoning depending on the brand you buy. The spicier the sausage, the spicier these appetizers will be.

Beef Bundles with Red Mustard Dip

½ pound lean ground beef
2 tablespoons sliced green onion
1 single-serving envelope *instant* tomato soup mix
¼ cup chopped water chestnuts
¼ teaspoon black pepper
⅛ teaspoon ground ginger

● In a skillet cook ground beef and sliced green onion till meat is brown and onion is tender; drain well. Stir in one envelope instant tomato soup mix, chopped water chestnuts, black pepper, ground ginger, and ¼ cup *water* till well combined.

1 17¼-ounce package (2 sheets) frozen puff pastry, thawed according to package directions

● Cut each pastry sheet into nine 3-inch squares. Put a rounded tablespoon of filling on each. Fold into triangles. Seal edges with fork. Place on a baking sheet. Cover; chill for 3 to 24 hours.

½ cup hot water
1 single-serving envelope *instant* tomato soup mix
2 tablespoons dry mustard
2 teaspoons paprika
1 tablespoon vinegar

● Bake pastries in a 400° oven about 15 minutes or till golden.
    For dip, combine hot water and one envelope instant tomato soup mix; cool. Combine with dry mustard and paprika; let stand 10 minutes. Stir in vinegar. If desired, garnish with tomato rose and parsley. Serve with pastries. Makes 18.

French, Chinese, and American cuisines are represented in these classy hors d'oeuvres. The French take credit for the puff pastry, the Chinese contribute the pungent mustard dip, and the Americans make them easier with the use of convenience products.

Guacamole

1 tablespoon chopped
   jalapeño *or* serrano
   peppers
2 medium avocados,
   seeded, peeled, and
   cut up
1 thin slice of a small onion
2 cloves garlic, minced
1 tablespoon lemon juice
¼ teaspoon salt

● See instructions on page 6 for handling chili peppers. In a blender container combine chili peppers, avocados, onion, garlic, lemon juice, and salt; cover and blend till well combined, stopping blender and scraping down sides occasionally. Transfer mixture to a bowl. Cover and chill till serving time. Makes 1¼ cups.

Jalapeño peppers give this creamy *Guacamole* its pep. Use it as a dip for tortilla chips or a smooth sauce for topping tacos, enchiladas, or other Mexican dishes. If you want it hotter, use the fresh serrano peppers.

Snappy Cocktail Nuts

3 tablespoons butter *or*
   margarine
2 teaspoons Worcestershire
   sauce
1 teaspoon chili powder *or*
   curry powder
1 teaspoon ground red
   pepper
⅛ teaspoon garlic powder
3 cups peanuts *or* cashews

● In a medium saucepan melt butter or margarine over medium heat. Stir in Worcestershire sauce, chili powder or curry powder, ground red pepper, and garlic powder till well mixed. Add peanuts or cashews, stirring till the nuts are evenly coated.

These nuts change identity as you change the seasoning. For a Mexican flavor, use chili powder; for a touch of India, use curry powder.

● Transfer mixture to a 13x9x2-inch baking pan. Bake in a 300° oven for 20 minutes, stirring twice. Let cool in the pan 15 minutes. Turn out onto paper towels to finish cooling. Makes 3 cups.

Avocado-Chicken Dip

Pictured on pages 8 and 9.

1 cup finely chopped
  cooked chicken *or*
  one 6¾-ounce can
  chunk-style chicken,
  drained and finely
  chopped
1 ripe medium avocado,
  seeded, peeled, and
  chopped
1 small tomato, seeded
  and chopped
¼ cup chopped onion
2 tablespoons rinsed,
  seeded, and chopped
  pickled jalapeño
  peppers
1 clove garlic, minced

● In a mixing bowl stir together the finely chopped cooked chicken or drained and finely chopped canned chicken, chopped avocado, seeded and chopped tomato, chopped onion, seeded and chopped pickled jalapeño peppers, and minced garlic.

This dip has all the ingredients of guacamole, and more. Sour cream gives it a creamy quality and chunks of chicken make it a dip you can sink your teeth into. After a few bites, you'll notice the heat from the jalapeños. You'll come to the conclusion that it's really not like guacamole at all. It's a notch above.

½ cup dairy sour cream
¼ cup milk
2 tablespoons mayonnaise
  or salad dressing
2 teaspoons lemon juice
¼ teaspoon dried oregano,
  crushed
⅛ teaspoon salt

● Stir in the sour cream, milk, mayonnaise or salad dressing, lemon juice, dried oregano, and salt. Stir till ingredients are thoroughly combined. Cover and chill till serving time.

Avocado slices (optional)
Oven-Crisp Tortilla Chips
  (see tip box, below) *or*
  tortilla chips

● If desired, garnish the dip with avocado slices. Serve with Oven-Crisp Tortilla Chips or other tortilla chips. Makes about 2¾ cups dip.

Oven-Crisp Tortilla Chips

Here's an easy way to make your own tortilla chips without frying them. Cut flour tortillas into wedges with kitchen shears or a knife. Place the wedges on an ungreased baking sheet and toast in a 350° oven for 10 to 12 minutes or till dry and crisp. You'll find they're sturdy for dipping, there's no messy cleanup, and the chips are lower in calories than those you buy in the store.

Texas Chili

Also pictured on the cover.

40	dried hot chili peppers *or* ¼ cup crushed red pepper
3	dried ancho peppers

● See instructions on page 6 for handling chili peppers. Crush hot chili peppers. Remove stems and seeds from ancho peppers; cut into 1-inch pieces. Place all peppers in a blender container. Cover; blend till ground.

2½	pounds beef round steak, cut into ½-inch cubes
2	tablespoons cooking oil
1	medium onion, chopped
2	cloves garlic, minced
1½	teaspoons ground cumin

● In a large saucepan brown *half* of the meat in hot oil. With a slotted spoon, remove meat; set aside. Add remaining meat, onion, garlic, cumin, and ground chili peppers; cook till meat is brown. Return all meat to saucepan.

1	10½-ounce can condensed beef broth
1	soup can (1⅓ cups) water
½	teaspoon dried oregano, crushed
	Hot cooked Pinto Beans

● Stir in beef broth, water, and oregano. Bring to boiling; reduce heat. Simmer, uncovered, for 1 to 1¼ hours or till meat is tender, stirring occasionally. Serve the chili with hot cooked Pinto Beans. Makes 6 to 8 servings.

● **Pinto Beans:** Rinse 1 pound (2½ cups) dry *pinto beans*. In a large saucepan or Dutch oven combine beans and 6 cups *water*. Cover and soak overnight. (Or, bring to boiling; reduce heat. Simmer 2 minutes. Remove from heat. Cover; let stand 1 hour.) Drain. In the same pan combine drained beans; 6 cups more *water*; 2 cloves *garlic*, minced; 1½ teaspoons *salt*; and ¼ teaspoon *black pepper*. Bring to boiling; reduce heat. Cover and simmer 1½ to 2 hours or till tender; drain. Makes 6 cups.

Texans are touchy about their chili. They use cubed beef instead of ground beef, and if they use beans they serve them with, not in, the chili. The chili's red color comes from pure ground chili peppers, not tomato. Texans seem to have a high tolerance for hot and spicy foods, so if you're not from the Lone Star state, taste at your own risk. In other words, "it'll knock your socks off!"

CHILI COOK-OFF

Pinto Beans

Texas Chili

Midwestern Butter Bean Chili *(see recipe, page 19)*

TNT Chili *(see recipe, page 18)*

TNT Chili

Pictured on page 17 and on the cover.

2 **pounds lean ground beef** 2 **medium onions, chopped** 1 **medium green pepper, seeded and chopped** 1 **stalk celery, chopped** 1 **clove garlic, minced**	● In a large saucepan or Dutch oven cook ground beef, onions, green pepper, celery, and garlic till meat is brown and vegetables are tender; do not drain.

2 **16-ounce cans tomatoes,
   cut up**
1 **15-ounce can tomato
   sauce**
1½ **cups water**
6 *or* **7 pickled jalapeño
   peppers, rinsed and
   chopped (½ cup)**
¼ **cup chili powder**
1 **tablespoon ground red
   pepper**
½ **teaspoon salt**
½ **teaspoon black pepper**
1 **bay leaf**
	● Stir in *undrained* tomatoes, tomato sauce, water, rinsed and chopped jalapeño peppers, chili powder, ground red pepper, salt, black pepper, and bay leaf. Bring mixture to boiling; reduce heat. Simmer, uncovered, for 1½ hours, stirring occasionally.

1 **15½-ounce can red kidney beans, drained**	● Stir in beans; cook 30 minutes more. Remove bay leaf before serving. Makes 8 to 10 servings.

Dynamite Chili: Prepare TNT Chili as directed above, *except* use 4 or 5 *pickled jalapeño peppers* (⅓ cup chopped) and 2 teaspoons *ground red pepper.*

Firecracker Chili: Prepare TNT Chili as directed above, *except* use 2 or 3 *pickled jalapeño peppers* (¼ cup chopped) and 1½ teaspoons *ground red pepper.*

Here's a chili you can gear up or down to suit your tolerance for explosives. *TNT, Dynamite,* and *Firecracker Chili* each contain ¼ *cup* of chili powder, but vary in the amounts of jalapeños and ground red pepper.

TNT Chili was judged "extra hot" by our panel of hot-food enthusiasts. One of the tasters began to sweat after a few bites. All of the panelists agreed that each bite was noticeably hotter, but enjoyed the chili down to the last spoonful.

Midwestern Butter Bean Chili

Pictured on page 17 and on the cover.

1 **pound ground pork**	● In a large skillet or a saucepan cook
1 **cup chopped onion**	pork, onion, and garlic till meat is brown
2 **cloves garlic, minced**	and onion is tender; drain off fat.

1 **16-ounce can tomatoes, cut up**
1 **16-ounce can butter beans** *or* **lima beans, drained**
1 **8-ounce can tomato sauce**
2 **4-ounce cans green chili peppers, rinsed, seeded, and chopped**
1 **tablespoon chili powder**
½ **teaspoon sugar**
½ **teaspoon salt**
½ **teaspoon dried basil, crushed**
¼ **teaspoon ground allspice**
¼ **teaspoon black pepper**
⅛ **teaspoon ground red pepper**

● Stir in *undrained* tomatoes; drained butter beans or lima beans; tomato sauce; rinsed, seeded, and chopped chili peppers; chili powder; sugar; salt; dried basil; ground allspice; black pepper; and ground red pepper. Bring mixture to boiling; reduce heat. Cover and simmer for 30 minutes. If desired, serve with toppings suggested in the tip box, below. Makes 4 to 6 servings.

Midwesterners will take liberties with chili that a Southwestern chili purist won't. This pork chili, for example, features big lima beans and a tomatoey broth that's mildly seasoned with green chili peppers, chili powder, basil, and allspice. Now that's real chili to lots of folks up north.

Favorite Chili Toppings

Everyone seems to have a different favorite food to top or stir into his bowl of chili. Heading the list are crushed crackers, shredded cheese, chopped carrot, sour cream, shredded lettuce, chopped onion, alfalfa sprouts, and chopped fresh tomato. All of these embellishments have one thing in common: They give your mouth a break from the spicy bite of the chili without overpowering the chili flavor.

Kitchen Sink Chili

2 slices bacon
1 pound lean ground beef
1 medium onion, chopped
1 stalk celery, chopped
2 cloves garlic, minced

● In a large saucepan or Dutch oven cook bacon slices till crisp. Remove, drain, and crumble bacon, reserving drippings in saucepan. Set bacon aside.
  Cook ground beef, onion, celery, and garlic in drippings till beef is brown and onion is tender; do not drain.

1 28-ounce can tomatoes, cut up
1 12-ounce can beer
1 tablespoon bottled hot pepper sauce
2 teaspoons chili powder
½ teaspoon salt
¼ teaspoon ground cinnamon

● Stir in *undrained* tomatoes, beer, bottled hot pepper sauce, chili powder, salt, and ground cinnamon. Bring to boiling; reduce heat. Simmer, uncovered, about 1 hour or to desired consistency, stirring occasionally.

1 15½-ounce can red kidney beans, drained
½ cup pimiento-stuffed olives, halved crosswise
½ cup raisins
1 square (1 ounce) unsweetened chocolate, cut up

● Stir in beans, olives, raisins, and chocolate. Simmer, uncovered, 5 minutes more or till chocolate is melted and mixture is heated through. Garnish with reserved crumbled bacon. Serves 6.

The ingredients in this relatively mild chili may seem a little out of the ordinary, but you'll be amazed (as we were) how tasty it really is.

Vegetarian Chili

2 tablespoons cooking oil
1½ cups chopped celery
1½ cups chopped green
    pepper
1 cup chopped onion
3 cloves garlic, minced

● In a large saucepan or Dutch oven heat oil. Add celery, green pepper, onion, and garlic. Cook, covered, till vegetables are tender but not brown.

2 28-ounce cans tomatoes,
    cut up
2 15½-ounce cans red
    kidney beans, drained
1 15-ounce can great
    northern beans *or* navy
    beans, drained
1 4-ounce can diced
    green chili peppers,
    drained
¼ cup vinegar
1 tablespoon chili powder
2 to 3 teaspoons bottled hot
    pepper sauce
2 teaspoons salt
1½ teaspoons dried basil,
    crushed
1½ teaspoons dried oregano,
    crushed
1½ teaspoons ground cumin
½ teaspoon ground allspice
½ teaspoon black pepper
1 bay leaf

● Stir in *undrained* tomatoes, drained red kidney beans, drained great northern or navy beans, drained diced green chili peppers, vinegar, chili powder, bottled hot pepper sauce, salt, dried basil, dried oregano, ground cumin, ground allspice, black pepper, and bay leaf. Bring the mixture to boiling; reduce heat and simmer, covered, for 1½ hours.

1 12-ounce can (1½ cups)
    beer
¾ cup peanuts *or* cashews
1 cup shredded Swiss,
    mozzarella *or* cheddar
    cheese (4 ounces)

● Stir in beer. Simmer, uncovered, 30 minutes more, or to desired consistency. Remove bay leaf. Stir in peanuts or cashews. Sprinkle shredded cheese atop each serving. Makes 8 servings.

Ever since Dave, our managing editor, introduced his spicy meatless chili recipe at a company potluck, it's been the inspiration for several variations. As in his popular recipe, protein comes from beans, nuts, and cheese instead of meat. The robust flavor comes from green chili peppers, bottled hot pepper sauce, and seven spices and herbs. Dave agrees that this chili is almost (but not quite) as hot and spicy as his original. He says if you want it hotter, add some crushed red pepper.

Use two forks to pull the cooked meat into shreds.

Place filling near one edge of tortilla and fold that edge up and over the filling.

Chow Down Chimichangas

Ingredients	Instructions
1 pound beef stew meat cut into 1½-inch cubes 1½ cups water 2 cloves garlic, minced ½ teaspoon salt	● In a medium saucepan combine meat, water, garlic, and salt. Bring to boiling; reduce heat. Cover and simmer about 1¼ hours or till meat is very tender. Uncover and boil rapidly for 10 to 12 minutes or till water has evaporated. Stir near end of cooking time to prevent meat from sticking. Remove from heat.
1 4-ounce can diced green chili peppers, drained 1 tablespoon vinegar 2 teaspoons chili powder ¼ teaspoon ground cumin Dash black pepper	● Shred the cooked meat with two forks, or let cool and pull apart with your fingers. Combine with chili peppers, vinegar, chili powder, cumin, and black pepper. (If making filling ahead, cover and chill up to three days. Heat till warm before filling tortillas.)
6 8- or 10-inch flour tortillas	● Meanwhile, stack tortillas and wrap in foil; heat in a 350° oven for 10 minutes. Spoon about ⅓ cup meat mixture onto each tortilla near one edge. Fold edge nearest filling up and over filling till mixture is almost covered. Fold in the two sides envelope-fashion, then roll up. Secure with wooden toothpicks.
Cooking oil	● In a heavy skillet or saucepan fry two or three filled tortillas in 1 inch hot cooking oil (375°) about 1 minute on each side or till golden brown. Drain on a rack or on paper towels. Keep warm in a 300° oven while frying remaining.
2 cups shredded lettuce Dairy sour cream Bottled picante sauce Pickled cherry peppers (optional)	● To serve, remove toothpicks. Place each chimichanga atop lettuce on a plate; top with sour cream and picante sauce. Garnish with pickled cherry peppers, if desired. Makes 6 servings.

Feature these beef-filled bundles at your next informal dinner party. Make them part of the fun by preparing the filling ahead and saving the assembling and frying until party time.

If you want to have them finished for your guests, fry the chimichangas and refrigerate or freeze them. To reheat, just wrap each bundle in foil and bake in a 350° oven until heated through: 15 to 20 minutes if refrigerated and 30 to 35 minutes if frozen.

Roll up and secure with
wooden toothpicks.

Fold in the two sides.

Chicken with Mole Sauce

2 dried ancho, mulato, *or* pasilla peppers *or* a combination of two varieties	● See instructions on page 6 for handling chili peppers and preparing dried chili peppers. Wash dried peppers in cold water; remove stems and seeds. Cut or tear the peppers into small pieces. Place in a bowl of boiling water; soak for 1 hour. Drain.
1 2½- to 3-pound broiler-fryer chicken, cut up Cooking oil	● Brush chicken with cooking oil. Place, skin side down, on the unheated rack of a broiler pan. Broil 5 to 6 inches from heat about 20 minutes or till lightly browned. Turn and broil 15 to 20 minutes more.
¾ cup chicken broth 1 medium tomato, peeled and sliced ¼ cup slivered almonds ¼ cup chopped onion 2 canned jalapeño peppers 2 tablespoons raisins 1 tablespoon sesame seed 1 clove garlic ⅛ teaspoon aniseed ⅛ teaspoon ground cinnamon ⅛ teaspoon ground coriander ⅛ teaspoon ground cloves 1 tablespoon cooking oil	● Meanwhile, for sauce, in a blender container combine chicken broth, sliced tomato, slivered almonds, chopped onion, jalapeño peppers, raisins, 1 tablespoon sesame seed, garlic clove, aniseed, ground cinnamon, ground coriander, ground cloves, and drained, soaked chili peppers. Cover the blender container; blend the broth mixture to a coarse puree. In a large skillet heat 1 tablespoon oil. Add the puree; cook over medium heat for 5 minutes, stirring occasionally.
½ square (½ ounce) unsweetened chocolate ¼ teaspoon sugar ⅛ teaspoon salt Dash black pepper	● Add chocolate, sugar, salt, and black pepper; cook and stir over low heat till chocolate is melted. Add chicken pieces; simmer, covered, for 10 minutes or till chicken is heated through. To serve, arrange chicken pieces on platter. Spoon sauce over chicken.
Toasted sesame seed	● Sprinkle with toasted sesame seed. Makes 6 servings.

Mexican legend has it that one day, when the nuns of the Santa Rosa convent had nothing to serve visiting dignitaries, they went to prayer. And while they prayed, they put everything they had on hand into a pot, including chili peppers, nuts, raisins, tomatoes, cinnamon, chocolate, and sesame seed. Their faith (and what great faith it must have been to serve such a dish) was rewarded with success and the richly seasoned mole (MO-lay) sauce was created. Today, mole sauces much like the one in this dish remain a traditional Southwestern favorite.

The specific dried pepper or combination of peppers you use will determine the flavor of the mole sauce. The ancho is the most widely used pepper in Mexican cooking. The mulato is slightly sweeter, though harder to find. Pasilla peppers are more piquant and slightly hotter than the ancho.

Chicken Enchiladas

¼ cup chopped pecans ¼ cup chopped onion 2 tablespoons butter *or* margarine	● In a skillet cook ¼ cup pecans and onion in butter or margarine till onion is tender and pecans are lightly toasted. Remove from heat.
1 3-ounce package cream cheese, softened 1 tablespoon milk ½ teaspoon salt ¼ teaspoon ground cumin 2 cups chopped cooked chicken	● In a bowl combine softened cream cheese, 1 tablespoon milk, salt, and ground cumin. Add nut mixture and chopped cooked chicken. Stir together till well combined.
6 8-inch flour tortillas	● Spoon about *⅓ cup* chicken mixture onto *each* tortilla near one edge; roll up. Place filled tortillas, seam side down, in a greased 12x7½x2-inch baking dish.
1 10¾-ounce can condensed cream of chicken soup 1 8-ounce carton dairy sour cream 1 cup milk 5 *or* 6 pickled jalapeño peppers, rinsed, seeded, and chopped (⅓ cup)	● In a bowl combine cream of chicken soup, sour cream, 1 cup milk, and the chopped pickled jalapeño peppers. Pour the soup mixture evenly over the tortillas in the baking dish. Cover with foil; bake in a 350° oven about 35 minutes or till heated through.
1 cup shredded Monterey Jack *or* cheddar cheese (4 ounces) 2 tablespoons chopped pecans	● Remove foil. Sprinkle enchiladas with cheese and 2 tablespoons pecans. Return to the 350° oven for 4 to 5 minutes or till cheese is melted. Makes 6 servings.

These nut-topped enchiladas are so rich and creamy that one of them makes an ample helping. Serve with a refreshing green or fruit salad and your favorite rice dish. Though the enchiladas are fairly mild, you may want to have a cold beverage handy to put out an occasional jalapeño fire.

Quesadillas with Picadillo Filling

2 tablespoons cooking oil 1 pound beef round steak, finely chopped ½ cup chopped onion 1 clove garlic, minced	● In a large skillet heat 2 tablespoons oil; cook beef, onion, and garlic till beef is brown and onion is tender.
2 medium tomatoes, peeled and chopped 1 medium apple, peeled, cored, and chopped ½ cup raisins 1 to 3 canned jalapeño peppers, drained and chopped 2 tablespoons vinegar 1 teaspoon sugar 1 teaspoon salt ½ teaspoon ground cinnamon ⅛ teaspoon ground cloves ⅛ teaspoon ground cumin	● Stir in tomatoes, apple, raisins, jalapeño peppers, vinegar, sugar, salt, cinnamon, cloves, and cumin; simmer, covered, for 20 minutes. 
½ cup toasted slivered almonds	● Stir in almonds; cook, uncovered, 2 minutes more. Remove from heat.
12 6-inch flour *or* corn tortillas 2 tablespoons cooking oil	● Place about ¼ *cup* filling on each tortilla. Fold tortillas in half; secure each with a wooden toothpick, if desired. In a skillet heat 2 tablespoons cooking oil; cook filled tortillas, a few at a time, in the hot oil about 2 minutes per side or till light brown. Keep warm in a 300° oven while frying remaining tortillas.
2 cups shredded lettuce Dairy sour cream Sliced green onions Radish roses	● To serve, place two quesadillas atop some of the shredded lettuce on a plate. Garnish with sour cream, green onions, and radish roses. Makes 6 servings.

Don't let the big words in the title put you off. Quesadillas (kay-sah-DEE-yahs) are made with flour or corn tortillas and are something between a turnover and a grilled sandwich.

  Picadillo (pee-kah-DEE-yoh) is a beef mixture made with tomato, onion, apple, raisins, nuts, and sweet spices. If you're not up to the heat of three jalapeños, use fewer jalapeños and remove the fiery ribs to which the pepper seeds are attached.

Fish Vera Cruz

1 pound fresh *or* frozen fish fillets 3 tablespoons all-purpose flour ¼ teaspoon salt ⅛ teaspoon black pepper 1 tablespoon cooking oil	● Thaw fish fillets, if frozen. Stir together the flour, salt, and black pepper. Coat fish fillets on both sides with the flour mixture. In a 10-inch skillet cook fish fillets in 1 tablespoon hot oil for 4 to 5 minutes per side or till fish flakes easily when tested with a fork. Remove fish from skillet; keep warm.
1 medium onion, sliced and separated into rings 1 clove garlic, minced 1 tablespoon cooking oil	● In the same skillet cook the sliced onion and minced garlic in 1 tablespoon hot cooking oil till the onion is tender but not brown.

1 16-ounce can tomatoes, cut up
¼ cup sliced pimiento-stuffed olives
¼ cup dry white wine
1 *or* 2 canned jalapeño peppers, rinsed, seeded, and chopped (1 tablespoon)
½ teaspoon sugar
1 small bay leaf
  Several dashes ground cinnamon
	● Stir in the *undrained* tomatoes, sliced olives, dry white wine, seeded and chopped jalapeño peppers, sugar, bay leaf, and cinnamon. Bring the mixture to boiling. Boil gently, uncovered, for 5 to 7 minutes or till the mixture is slightly thickened.
	  Add the cooked fish fillets to the tomato mixture; heat through. Remove the bay leaf.

Hot cooked rice	● Arrange the fish on a platter; spoon sauce over fish. Serve with hot cooked rice. Makes 4 servings.

Of the recipes inspired by the bounty of Mexico's coastal waters, one of the most popular there is fish prepared Vera Cruz-style. Fish fillets are fried, then smothered in a tomato sauce rich with onion, garlic, jalapeño peppers, and cinnamon. Flavor this good is hard to keep under a sombrero and has hooked many across the border as well.

Tex-Mex for Six

Update the flavors of Old Mexico with the creative cooking style of today's Southwest. Because many of the foods can be made ahead, this elegant menu will impress your guests without leaving you exhausted.

MENU
Avocado Soup
Fiesta Chicken Roll-Ups
Spinach Salad with
  Garbanzo Beans
Flour tortillas
Almond Dessert
Pot Coffee con Leche

MENU COUNTDOWN

6 Hours Ahead or Day Before:
Prepare Avocado Soup; chill.
Prepare salad dressing; chill.
Pound and roll boned chicken breasts for Fiesta Chicken Roll-Ups; cover and chill.

1½ Hours Ahead:
Assemble vegetables for salad; chill. Coat, brown, and bake chicken and begin sauce for Fiesta Chicken Roll-Ups. Assemble ingredients for Almond Dessert. Dissolve brown sugar for Pot Coffee con Leche.

5 Minutes Ahead:
Wrap tortillas in foil; heat in a 400° oven. Drizzle dressing over salad; toss. Finish sauce for Fiesta Chicken Roll-Ups; pour over chicken.

During or After Meal:
Bake Almond Dessert. Steep Pot Coffee con Leche.

Almond Dessert
(see recipe, page 32)

Spinach Salad with Garbanzo Beans
(see recipe, page 30)

Avocado Soup
(see recipe, page 30)

Pot Coffee con Leche
(see recipe, page 33)

Fiesta Chicken Roll-Ups
(see recipe, page 31)

Avocado Soup

Pictured on page 28.

1 14½-ounce can chicken
   broth
2 medium avocados, seeded,
   peeled, and cut up
1 thin slice of a small onion
3 tablespoons lime juice
½ teaspoon salt

● In a blender container combine chicken broth, avocados, onion slice, lime juice, and salt; cover the blender container and blend till the mixture is smooth. Pour into a bowl.

1½ cups milk
1 lime, cut into wedges
   (optional)

● Stir in milk. Cover and chill thoroughly. If desired, serve with lime wedges. Makes 6 servings.

Soup usually is the first course of a large Mexican meal. Start your special dinner with this easy, creamy soup that you whirl in the blender. Make it ahead of time and chill it in the refrigerator until you're ready to serve.

Spinach Salad with Garbanzo Beans

Pictured on pages 28 and 29.

3 tablespoons olive oil
2 tablespoons white wine
   vinegar
1 tablespoon water
1 clove garlic, minced
½ teaspoon salt
½ teaspoon brown sugar
¼ teaspoon dry mustard
¼ teaspoon dried thyme,
   crushed

● For dressing, in a screw-top jar combine oil, white wine vinegar, water, garlic, salt, brown sugar, dry mustard, and thyme. Cover and shake well. (To store dressing, chill in the refrigerator; let stand at room temperature about 30 minutes before serving.)

6 cups torn fresh spinach
   (8 ounces)
1 15-ounce can garbanzo
   beans, drained
½ cup sliced radishes

● In a large bowl combine spinach, garbanzo beans, and radishes. Shake dressing and pour over salad; toss lightly to coat. Makes 6 servings.

Tossed salads, as Americans know them, are not common to most Mexican meals. Instead, garnishes of chopped lettuce, radishes, and onion usually replace the need for added greens. Salad-loving gringos, however, will find this salad a refreshing and fitting complement to the rest of the meal.

Fiesta Chicken Roll-Ups

Pictured on page 29.

3 whole large chicken breasts, skinned, halved lengthwise, and boned	● For each chicken roll, place a chicken breast half between two pieces of clear plastic wrap. Working from center to edge, use smooth side of a meat mallet to pound lightly to ⅛-inch thickness.
1 4-ounce can whole green chili peppers, rinsed and drained	● Remove wrap. Halve *three* peppers lengthwise; remove seeds. (Keep any remaining peppers for another use.) Place one pepper half on each chicken piece, as shown. Fold in sides of chicken; roll up jelly-roll style. Secure with wooden toothpicks. If desired, cover and chill several hours or overnight.
¼ cup all-purpose flour **¼ cup yellow cornmeal** **Dash garlic powder** **Dash ground red pepper** **1 egg** **3 tablespoons milk**	● Combine ¼ cup flour, cornmeal, garlic powder, ground red pepper, and ¼ teaspoon *salt;* set aside. Beat together egg and 3 tablespoons milk. Roll each chicken roll in flour mixture; dip in egg mixture, then roll again in flour mixture.
¼ cup cooking oil	● In a skillet heat ¼ cup oil over medium heat. Cook chicken rolls in hot oil 10 to 15 minutes, turning to brown all sides. Transfer chicken to a 12x7½x2-inch baking dish. Bake in a 400° oven 15 to 17 minutes or till tender.
3 tablespoons cooking oil **2 tablespoons finely chopped onion** **2 cloves garlic, minced**	● Meanwhile, prepare sauce. In a 2-quart saucepan heat 3 tablespoons oil. Add onion and garlic; cook about 5 minutes or till tender but not brown.
1 7½-ounce can tomatoes, cut up **½ cup chicken broth** **2 tablespoons chili powder** **2 teaspoons vinegar** **¾ teaspoon crushed red pepper** **¼ teaspoon ground cumin** **¼ teaspoon dried oregano, crushed**	● Stir in the *undrained* tomatoes, chicken broth, chili powder, vinegar, crushed red pepper, ground cumin, dried oregano, and ¼ teaspoon *salt.* Simmer the mixture, uncovered, for 20 minutes. Transfer the baked chicken rolls to a serving platter. Remove toothpicks; keep chicken warm.
½ cup milk **2 tablespoons all-purpose flour**	● Combine ½ cup milk and 2 tablespoons flour; stir into tomato mixture. Cook and stir till thickened and bubbly. Cook and stir 1 minute more.
½ cup shredded Monterey Jack *or* cheddar cheese **¼ cup sliced pitted ripe olives**	● To serve, pour sauce over chicken rolls; top with cheese and olives. Makes 6 servings.

The green chili peppers hidden inside these chicken rolls are mild, so you can serve this impressive entrée to both torrid and tender palates. If everyone at the table has a high tolerance for hot food, consider using green chili peppers that have "hot" on the label.

Place half of a seeded chili pepper on each pounded piece of chicken. If the chili peppers are too long, you may have to fold them under to keep them inside when you roll up the chicken.

Almond Dessert

Pictured on page 28.

1 cup slivered almonds	● Spread almonds in a single layer in a baking pan. Toast in a 350° oven about 10 minutes or till light brown, stirring often. Reserve *1 tablespoon*. Place remainder in a blender container. Cover and grind till fine; set aside.
¼ cup butter *or* margarine 1¾ cups sugar ¾ cup water 3 inches stick cinnamon	● In a 1½-quart saucepan melt butter or margarine. Add sugar, water, and stick cinnamon; boil gently, uncovered, for 5 minutes. Remove from heat. Remove and discard stick cinnamon.
¼ cup dark rum	● Pour *half* of the sugar and butter mixture (about 1 cup) into a small bowl. Stir in the rum; set aside.
2 eggs	● Beat eggs slightly with a fork; mix into remaining half of the sugar and butter mixture. Stir in the ground toasted almonds. Return to heat. Cook and stir over low heat for 4 to 5 minutes or till thickened. Remove from heat.
1 10¾-ounce frozen loaf pound cake, thawed	● Cut pound cake crosswise into 18 slices about ½ inch thick. Dip 6 of the cake slices in the rum mixture and place on the bottom of an 8x8x2-inch baking dish. Spoon *one-third* of the almond mixture over cake slices. Repeat dipping and layering till there are 3 layers of cake and 3 layers of almond mixture. Bake, uncovered, in a 350° oven for 15 to 20 minutes or till light brown. Cool slightly.
½ cup dairy sour cream ¼ cup milk	● Combine sour cream and milk. Cut baked dessert into serving pieces and place on individual plates. Top with sour cream mixture and reserved toasted almonds. Makes 6 servings.

Now for the perfect end to a perfect meal. Soak pound cake slices in rum-flavored syrup, layer with a ground almond mixture, and bake. For a crowning touch, top each rich serving with a satiny spoonful of sour cream topping and a sprinkling of toasted almonds.

Pot Coffee

Pictured on page 29.

6 cups water
¼ cup packed brown sugar
3 inches stick cinnamon
6 whole cloves

● In a 3-quart saucepan combine water, brown sugar, stick cinnamon, and cloves; heat and stir till sugar is dissolved.

¾ cup regular-grind, roasted coffee

● Add coffee. Bring to boiling; reduce heat. Simmer, uncovered, for 1 to 2 minutes. Remove from heat. Cover and let stand 15 minutes. Strain before serving. Makes 6 (8-ounce) servings.

Pot Coffee con Leche: Pour equal amounts of *Pot Coffee* and *warm milk* into each cup. Add sugar to taste.

Ignore your percolator or coffee maker when brewing this traditional Mexican coffee. Steep the coffee and spices with water in a saucepan and strain before serving. If the strainer you use does not have a fine mesh, line the inside of the strainer with several layers of cheesecloth to keep the coffee grounds from seeping through the holes.

Make Your Own Flour Tortillas

Like homemade bread, homemade flour tortillas taste fresher than tortillas from the supermarket. What's more, they're as easy to make as biscuits.

Stir together 2 cups *all-purpose flour*, 1 teaspoon *salt*, and 1 teaspoon *baking powder*. Cut in 2 tablespoons *shortening* till mixture resembles cornmeal. Gradually add ½ to ¾ cup *warm water*; mix till the dough forms a ball. Knead 15 to 20 times. Let stand 15 minutes.

Divide dough into 12 equal portions. Shape into balls. On a lightly floured surface or between two pieces of waxed paper, roll each ball into a 7-inch circle. Cook on a medium-hot ungreased griddle or skillet about 20 seconds or till puffy. Turn and cook about 20 seconds more or till edges curl slightly. Makes 12.

Italian Beef Rolls

1½ **pounds beef round steak cut ¼ inch thick**
½ **cup cooking oil**
⅓ **cup red wine vinegar**
1 **clove garlic, crushed**
1 **teaspoon dried thyme, crushed**
½ **teaspoon sugar**
½ **teaspoon celery salt**
½ **teaspoon dry mustard**
½ **teaspoon dried oregano, crushed**
½ **teaspoon black pepper**
¼ **teaspoon bottled hot pepper sauce**

● Cut round steak into 6 equal portions. Pound to ⅛-inch thickness. Place the steak portions in a shallow baking dish.

For marinade, combine cooking oil, red wine vinegar, 1 clove garlic, thyme, ½ teaspoon sugar, celery salt, dry mustard, oregano, black pepper, and bottled hot pepper sauce. Pour the marinade over the meat.

Cover; marinate 1 hour at room temperature or overnight in the refrigerator, turning the meat occasionally.

½ **pound bulk Italian sausage**
2 **tablespoons chopped onion**
2 **tablespoons chopped green pepper**

● For filling, in a skillet cook sausage, onion, and green pepper over medium heat till sausage is brown; drain off fat. Cool filling slightly.

Drain round steak, reserving marinade. Place a scant *¼ cup* of filling on one of the narrow ends of *each* steak. Fold in sides, as shown at top; roll up jelly-roll style. Secure with wooden toothpicks or string, as shown at bottom. Place *medium* coals around drip pan. Place beef rolls on grill over drip pan. Lower hood. Grill 35 to 45 minutes or till done; brush occasionally with marinade.

1 **14-ounce can peeled Italian-style tomatoes, cut up**
1 **clove garlic, minced**
½ **teaspoon sugar**
¼ **teaspoon salt**
¼ **teaspoon dried basil, crushed**
¼ **teaspoon crushed red pepper**
1 **tablespoon cold water**
2 **teaspoons cornstarch**

● Meanwhile, for sauce, in a medium saucepan combine *undrained* tomatoes, 1 clove garlic, ½ teaspoon sugar, salt, basil, and crushed red pepper. Simmer, covered, for 10 minutes. Stir cold water into cornstarch; stir into sauce. Cook and stir till thickened and bubbly; cook and stir 2 minutes more.

Before serving, remove the toothpicks or string from the beef rolls; serve with sauce. Makes 6 servings.

Here's a grilling idea that's impressive yet economical. This mildly seasoned dish can be made more or less spicy depending on the heat level of the sausage you use for the filling.

Pound steak pieces with a meat mallet to tenderize; marinate. Place filling on steak pieces; fold in sides.

Roll up meat, enclosing the filling. Secure meat roll with string.

Tropical Kabobs

⅓ cup cooking oil ⅓ cup lemon juice 2 tablespoons curry powder 1 tablespoon chopped fresh mint 1 teaspoon bottled hot pepper sauce ¼ teaspoon grated orange peel ¼ teaspoon ground red pepper	● For marinade, in a screw-top jar combine cooking oil, lemon juice, curry powder, chopped fresh mint, bottled hot pepper sauce, grated orange peel, and ground red pepper. Cover the jar tightly; shake well to mix.	**Bring the Caribbean to your dinner table with the delightful flavors of pineapple, citrus, coconut, curry, and fresh mint. (If you can't get fresh mint, use ¾ teaspoon dried mint flakes, crushed.) To toast coconut, spread a thin layer in a shallow baking pan. Bake in a 350° oven for 6 to 7 minutes or till lightly browned. Stir once or twice during baking for even browning.**
1 pound boneless pork, cut into 1½-inch cubes	● Place meat in a plastic bag in a deep bowl. Pour marinade over meat; close bag. Marinate in refrigerator 8 hours or overnight, turning meat occasionally. Drain meat, reserving marinade.	
12 chicken wings 1 small pineapple, peeled, cored, and cut into 1½-inch chunks 1 medium green *or* sweet red pepper (*or* a combination), cut into 1½-inch pieces 12 cherry tomatoes	● Alternately thread meat cubes, chicken wings, pineapple chunks, and green or red pepper pieces onto skewers. Grill over *hot* coals for 10 to 15 minutes, turning frequently. Add cherry tomatoes; grill 5 minutes more, brushing with reserved marinade.	
¼ cup toasted coconut	● To serve, sprinkle kabobs with toasted coconut. Makes 6 servings.	

Fiery Hot Country Ribs

4 pounds country-style pork
    ribs

- In a large saucepan or Dutch oven cook ribs, covered, in enough boiling salted water to cover for 45 to 60 minutes or till ribs are tender; drain well.

1 small onion, chopped
1 clove garlic, minced
1 tablespoon cooking oil
1 14-ounce bottle (1½ cups)
    catsup
⅓ cup vinegar
¼ cup molasses
1 tablespoon bottled hot
    pepper sauce
2 teaspoons ground red
    pepper
1 teaspoon chili powder
½ teaspoon salt
½ teaspoon dry mustard

- Meanwhile, for sauce, in a medium saucepan cook onion and garlic in hot cooking oil till the onion is tender but not brown. Stir in catsup, vinegar, molasses, bottled hot pepper sauce, ground red pepper, chili powder, salt, and dry mustard. Bring the mixture to boiling; reduce heat. Simmer, uncovered, for 15 minutes, stirring occasionally.

- Grill ribs over *slow* coals for 45 minutes, turning every 15 minutes. Brush with sauce frequently. If desired, heat any remaining sauce and serve with ribs. Makes 6 servings.

Each time we tested this recipe, we were wild about the flavor, but we wanted it hotter. When the comments for the final test were "Good and hot!" and "Nice kick!" we suspected we had a winner.

   Just to be sure, we subjected the recipe to our panel of tasters who like extra-hot food. They agreed that these ribs are sensational. They offered one caution: the ribs are hot at first bite (and first whiff) and get hotter the more you eat!

Apple-Herb Rib Roast

2½ teaspoons fennel seed 2 teaspoons dried celery flakes 2 teaspoons dried oregano 2 teaspoons dried basil 1½ teaspoons dried rosemary 1 teaspoon onion salt ½ teaspoon salt ½ teaspoon garlic powder ½ teaspoon ground red pepper ¼ teaspoon dried sage leaves ¼ teaspoon black pepper	● In a blender container place fennel seed, dried celery flakes, dried oregano, dried basil, dried rosemary, onion salt, salt, garlic powder, ground red pepper, dried sage leaves, and black pepper; cover the blender container. Grind the spices to a fine powder. Empty the spice mixture into a small bowl.
4 teaspoons cooking oil	● Stir the oil into the spice mixture to form a paste.
1 4-pound pork loin center rib roast, backbone loosened 1 large cooking apple, cored and cut into thin wedges	● Place roast rib side down. Cut pockets in roast from meaty side between rib bones. Rub spice mixture evenly into each pocket. Insert 2 apple wedges into each pocket. Tie roast together lengthwise twice, making the ties about 1½ inches apart.
1 5½-ounce can (⅔ cup) apple juice Fresh sage (optional)	*To grill,* insert spit rod through center of roast. Adjust holding forks and test balance. Insert meat thermometer near center of roast, not touching either spit rod or bone. Place *medium-hot* coals around drip pan. Attach spit; position drip pan under meat. Turn on motor. Lower grill hood. Roast over *medium-hot* coals for 1½ to 2 hours or till meat thermometer registers 170° for well done. Brush roast with apple juice occasionally during the last 30 minutes. 　Remove ties from roast before serving. Carve roast, as shown. Garnish with fresh sage, if desired. Makes 6 servings. 　*To roast in oven,* place pockets upward on rack in a shallow roasting pan. Insert meat thermometer into center of roast, not touching bone. Roast in a 325° oven, uncovered, for 1¾ to 2½ hours or till meat thermometer registers 170°. Brush occasionally with apple juice during the last 30 minutes of roasting.

For easier carving, be sure to have the butcher loosen the backbone from the rib bones. At home, cut pockets in the roast between each of the rib bones to hold the herb and oil mixture and apple slices. As the meat roasts, the herb mixture penetrates the meat and the apple lends a subtle sweetness. Brushing occasionally with apple juice makes the outer surface brown and crisp.

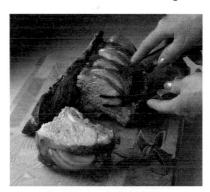

To carve the roast, slice lengthwise along the backbone to separate the meat from the bone. Then slice crosswise directly next to the rib bones to make chops, leaving the backbone intact.

Moroccan Stew

1 **pound lamb *or* pork stew meat, cut into 1-inch cubes**	● In a 10-inch skillet brown meat and onion in hot oil.
½ **cup chopped onion**	
2 **tablespoons cooking oil**	

3 **tablespoons all-purpose flour**	● Stir the flour into the meat mixture in the skillet. Stir in the *undrained* cut-up tomatoes, water, ground ginger, ground cumin, ground cinnamon, sugar, salt, and black pepper.
1 **16-ounce can tomatoes, cut up**	
¼ **cup water**	
1 **teaspoon ground ginger**	Transfer the meat mixture to a 2-quart casserole. Bake, covered, in a 325° oven for 30 minutes.
1 **teaspoon ground cumin**	
1 **teaspoon ground cinnamon**	
½ **teaspoon sugar**	
½ **teaspoon salt**	
½ **teaspoon black pepper**	

1 **15-ounce can garbanzo beans, drained**	● Stir in garbanzo beans, green beans, and carrots; cover and bake 1 hour more. Serve with pita bread. Makes 4 to 6 servings.
1 **cup frozen cut green beans**	
½ **cup sliced carrots**	
Pita bread rounds	

North African cooks are not timid in their use of spices and herbs. However, their dishes are generally easy on the tongue, as is this one.

Just as essential as spices to the enjoyment of an African stew is the presence of bread. In Morocco, bread is used in place of spoons to soak up the liquids and lift morsels to the mouth.

Mulligatawny Stew

1	5- to 6-pound stewing chicken
4½	cups water
1	large onion, cut up
2	carrots, cut up
1	teaspoon salt

● In a large saucepan place chicken, water, cut-up onion, cut-up carrots, and salt. Bring to boiling; reduce heat. Cover and simmer for 2 hours or till the chicken is tender.

1	cup chopped onion
4	cloves garlic, minced
2	tablespoons cooking oil
1	tablespoon ground coriander
1½	teaspoons ground cumin
½	teaspoon turmeric
½	teaspoon ground red pepper

● Meanwhile, in a small skillet cook chopped onion and garlic in hot cooking oil for 5 minutes. Add ground coriander, ground cumin, turmeric, and ground red pepper; cook and stir over medium heat 2 minutes more.

● Remove chicken from broth. When chicken is cool enough to handle, remove and discard skin and bones; chop chicken. Remove and discard vegetables. Skim fat from broth. Return chicken to broth. Stir in onion and spice mixture. Cover; simmer 30 minutes.

⅓	cup whipping cream
3	tablespoons all-purpose flour
1	tablespoon grated gingerroot

● Stir cream into flour (mixture will be thick); stir into stew. Add gingerroot. Cook over medium heat, stirring constantly, till thickened and bubbly. Cook and stir 1 to 2 minutes more.

Snipped fresh coriander *or* parsley
1 lemon, cut into wedges

● To serve, ladle the stew into individual serving bowls. Garnish each serving with snipped fresh coriander or parsley. Accompany each serving with a wedge of lemon to be squeezed into the stew just before eating. Makes 8 servings.

As the story goes, mulligatawny soup was first prepared by local cooks in southern India for their English masters. The literal meaning, "pepper water," betrays its delicate flavor. Our version of the soup is so hearty we called it stew.

Two forms of coriander are used in this recipe. Coriander seed is available in most grocery stores whole or ground. Some say it tastes like lemon and sage. It is used extensively in Indian cooking and is an important ingredient in curry powder. Aromatic coriander leaves resemble parsley in appearance and often are used to garnish Indian dishes. Also called cilantro or Chinese parsley, these leaves are sold in Indian, Oriental, and Mexican markets.

Place a tortilla on top of the hot oil. Using a metal ladle, press the tortilla against the bottom of the pan for 40 to 60 seconds or till tortilla is golden and forms a bowl around the ladle. With tongs, remove tortilla; drain on a rack or on paper towels.

Mexican Chicken Soup in Tortilla Bowls

Cooking oil *or* shortening for deep-fat frying
6 5½-inch corn *or* flour tortillas

2 cups milk
1 10¾-ounce can condensed cream of chicken soup
1 8¾-ounce can whole kernel corn, drained
1 cup chopped tomatoes
1 4-ounce can diced green chili peppers, drained
2 tablespoons minced dried onion
2 cloves garlic, minced
¾ teaspoon dried oregano, crushed
½ teaspoon ground red pepper
1½ cups cubed cooked chicken
1 cup shredded Monterey Jack cheese (4 ounces)
Cherry tomatoes, halved (optional)
Parsley (optional)

● To make tortilla bowls, in a saucepan or deep-fat fryer heat about 2½ inches oil or shortening to 375°. Fry one tortilla at a time, using instructions at far left.

● For soup, in a large saucepan stir together milk and condensed soup; stir in corn, tomatoes, chili peppers, dried onion, garlic, oregano, and ground red pepper. Bring to boiling; reduce heat. Simmer, uncovered, for 5 minutes.

Add chicken and cheese; heat and stir till cheese is melted and chicken is heated through. To serve, place each tortilla bowl in a soup bowl; fill with soup. Garnish with cherry tomatoes and parsley, if desired. Makes 6 servings.

Instead of serving tortilla chips with your soup, serve the soup in a tortilla! Regular corn tortillas become crispy soup bowls when you fry them in hot oil for a minute or less. For softer shells, use flour tortillas. The quick and easy soup makes up for the extra effort you put into making the bowls.

Groundnut Beef Stew

1 pound beef stew meat, cut into 1-inch cubes 1 tablespoon cooking oil	● In a Dutch oven brown *half* of the meat in hot oil; remove. Repeat with remaining meat.
1 16-ounce can tomatoes, cut up ½ cup water 1½ to 2 teaspoons crushed red pepper ½ teaspoon salt ½ teaspoon instant beef bouillon granules	● Return all of the meat to the Dutch oven; add *undrained* tomatoes, water, crushed red pepper, salt, and instant beef bouillon granules. Cover and simmer for 1½ hours.
⅓ cup creamy peanut butter 1 medium sweet potato, peeled and cut into ½-inch slices 1 small onion, cut into wedges 1 small green pepper, cut into 1-inch pieces	● Stir peanut butter into beef mixture. Add sweet potato, onion, and green pepper. Bring to boiling; reduce heat. Cover and simmer for 15 to 20 minutes or till vegetables are tender. Makes 4 to 6 servings.

Peanuts are known as groundnuts in West Africa. Like Americans, West Africans prize them for their flavor and protein content. Peanuts in the form of peanut butter account for this stew's nutty flavor and interesting texture.

Crushed red pepper is often used to intensify the flavor of West African peanut sauces. Use your discretion to decide how much of the pepper you will add to this stew.

Chinese Soup Bowl

¼ pound boneless pork
2 tablespoons red wine
     vinegar
1 tablespoon cornstarch
1 tablespoon dry sherry
2 teaspoons soy sauce
¾ teaspoon Red Pepper Oil
     (see recipe, page 92) *or*
     chili oil
½ teaspoon black pepper
	● Partially freeze meat; thinly slice across the grain into bite size strips that are ¼ inch thick.
	   In a bowl combine red wine vinegar, cornstarch, sherry, soy sauce, Red Pepper Oil or chili oil, and black pepper. Add pork strips, stirring to coat; let stand at room temperature 20 to 30 minutes.

4 dried black mushrooms ½ cup warm water	● Soak mushrooms in warm water for 30 minutes; drain. Slice mushrooms into thin strips, discarding stems; set aside.

1 8-ounce package fresh
     bean curd (tofu), cut
     into ¼-inch cubes (2
     cups)
1 tablespoon cooking oil
2 14½-ounce cans chicken
     broth
¼ cup shredded carrot
	● Drain meat, reserving marinade. In a saucepan brown meat and tofu in cooking oil. Add chicken broth, carrot, and reserved mushrooms. Simmer, covered, for 5 minutes.

¼ cup pea pods, thinly bias sliced	● Stir in reserved marinade. Cook and stir over medium heat till thickened and bubbly. Add pea pods. Cook and stir 2 minutes more.
1 egg 1 green onion, thinly sliced	● In a small dish beat egg slightly with a fork; slowly add to soup, stirring gently. Immediately remove from heat. Sprinkle with green onion. Makes 4 servings.

Some of the ingredients in this soup may be unfamiliar to you, but they are commonplace in a Chinese kitchen.
● **Chili oil** is sesame oil infused with the heat and color of hot red chili peppers. You can buy it in Oriental markets or make your own using the recipe for Red Pepper Oil on page 92.
● **Dried black mushrooms** have a darker skin and more pronounced flavor than fresh white mushrooms. Before cooking, soften them by soaking in warm water. You can buy them in Oriental markets.
● **Bean curd,** also known as tofu, has little flavor of its own but takes on the flavor of the foods it is mixed with. It is available in the produce section of many supermarkets.

Cajun Occasion

Cajuns are former French-Canadians who resettled in the Louisiana bayous. They are a friendly and exuberant people who enjoy the simple pleasures of fellowship, festive music, and richly seasoned food. This easy menu not only gives you a taste of Cajun tradition, but also lets you spend most of your time where you belong—with your guests.

MENU
Wine Sparkler
Seafood Étouffée
Purchased French bread
Garden Salad Vinaigrette
Purchased pecan pie

MENU COUNTDOWN
1½ Hours Ahead:
Prepare dressing and assemble vegetables for Garden Salad Vinaigrette; cover and chill. Begin cooking Seafood Étouffée. Prepare Wine Sparkler.

5 Minutes Ahead:
Slice French bread. Remove pecan pie from refrigerator; bring to room temperature. Drizzle dressing over Garden Salad Vinaigrette; toss. Add shrimp to Seafood Étouffée; finish cooking.

Garden Salad Vinaigrette
(see recipe, page 47)

Seafood Étouffée
(see recipe, page 46)

Wine Sparkler
(see recipe, page 47)

Seafood Étouffée

Pictured on pages 44 and 45.

12 ounces fresh *or* frozen peeled and deveined shrimp ½ cup butter *or* margarine ½ cup all-purpose flour	● Thaw shrimp, if frozen. In a heavy large saucepan melt butter or margarine. Stir in the flour. Cook over medium-low heat, *stirring constantly*, for 20 to 30 minutes or till a dark reddish-brown roux is formed, as shown.
1 10-ounce can tomatoes and green chili peppers 1¾ cups water 2 carrots, cut into ¼-inch slices 1 stalk celery, cut into ½-inch slices ½ cup chopped onion ½ cup chopped green pepper 1 teaspoon dried basil, crushed ½ teaspoon salt ½ to ¾ teaspoon ground red pepper ¼ teaspoon black pepper	● Stir in the *undrained* tomatoes and green chili peppers, water, sliced carrots, sliced celery, chopped onion, chopped green pepper, dried basil, salt, ground red pepper, and black pepper. Bring the mixture to boiling, stirring frequently; reduce heat. Cover the saucepan and simmer about 25 minutes or till the vegetables are tender.
1 6-ounce can crab meat, drained, flaked, and cartilage removed 3 cups hot cooked rice	● Add shrimp and crab meat. Bring to boiling; reduce heat. Simmer, uncovered, for 1 to 3 minutes or till shrimp turns pink. Serve in bowls with a mound of rice atop each serving. Makes 6 servings.

An étouffée (A-too-FAY) is a type of stew in which shellfish is smothered in a seasoned vegetable mixture and served with rice. The dish begins with a roux (rhymes with stew), a cooked mixture of butter and flour. A Cajun will tell you to cook the roux till it turns the color of an old copper penny. Then you're sure the stew will have the rich look and taste that Cajun cooking is famous for.

Garden Salad Vinaigrette

Pictured on page 44.

¼ cup white wine vinegar
2 tablespoons water
2 tablespoons salad oil
1½ teaspoons sugar
¾ teaspoon celery seed
¼ teaspoon dry mustard
¼ teaspoon salt
⅛ teaspoon ground red
   pepper

● For dressing, in a screw-top jar combine white wine vinegar, water, salad oil, sugar, celery seed, dry mustard, salt, and ground red pepper. Cover and shake well. (To store dressing, chill in the refrigerator.)

To keep the sliced avocados from turning brown, toss the slices with a little of the salad dressing before adding them to the salad.

1 small head Bibb lettuce,
   torn into pieces
1 small red onion, sliced
   and separated into rings
2 avocados, seeded,
   peeled, and sliced
1 cucumber, halved
   lengthwise and sliced
½ cup sliced radishes

● In a large bowl combine lettuce, onion, avocados, cucumber, and radishes. Shake the dressing well and pour over salad. Toss lightly to coat. Makes 6 servings.

Wine Sparkler

Pictured on page 45.

1 1-liter bottle rosé wine
1 6-ounce can frozen pink
   lemonade concentrate,
   thawed
2 10-ounce bottles (2½
   cups) carbonated water,
   chilled
   Ice cubes
6 lemon slices

● In a pitcher combine the wine and the lemonade concentrate. If making ahead of time, cover and chill.
   Just before serving stir in the chilled carbonated water. Serve over ice cubes in glasses. Garnish with lemon slices. Makes 6 (10-ounce) servings.

Serve this light and tangy beverage with the meal or hand your guests a glass to enjoy before dinner. When they're down to the last few sips, slip into the kitchen and put the finishing touches on the étouffée.

Javanese Ham and Pineapple Curry

Javanese Ham and Pineapple Curry

1	medium onion, chopped
1	clove garlic, minced
1	teaspoon grated gingerroot
2	tablespoons butter *or* margarine
2	tablespoons curry powder

● In a saucepan cook onion, garlic, and gingerroot in butter or margarine till onion is tender but not brown. Stir in curry powder; cook 1 minute more.

2	tablespoons all-purpose flour
1	8-ounce can pineapple chunks (juice pack)
1	cup chicken broth
2	medium carrots, sliced
1	tablespoon catsup

● Stir in flour. Drain juice (⅓ cup) from pineapple chunks; set chunks aside. Add juice, chicken broth, carrots, and catsup to curry mixture. Bring to boiling; reduce heat. Cover and simmer 15 minutes.

2	cups cubed fully cooked ham
	Toasted coconut (optional)
	Hot cooked rice

● Stir in ham and reserved pineapple chunks; heat through. Transfer to a serving bowl. If desired, garnish with toasted coconut. Serve with hot cooked rice. Makes 4 servings.

"Java," wrote Marco Polo, "is a very rich island, producing . . . all the precious spices that can be found in the world." The food from the central region of this Indonesian island unites the flavors of sweet, sour, and hot. Capture the essence of Javanese cuisine using ingredients commonly found in American kitchens.

Curried Tuna and Tomatoes
(see recipe, page 50)

Chicken Vindaloo
(see recipe, page 51)

Curried Tuna and Tomatoes

Pictured on pages 48 and 49.

1 large onion, chopped 2 cloves garlic, minced 1 teaspoon grated gingerroot *or* ¼ teaspoon ground ginger 3 tablespoons butter *or* margarine	● In a saucepan cook the chopped onion, garlic, and grated gingerroot or ground ginger in butter or margarine till onion is tender.
2 tablespoons curry powder 2 teaspoons chili powder	● Stir in curry powder and chili powder; cook and stir 2 minutes more.
3 tablespoons all-purpose flour 1½ cups chicken broth 1 7½-ounce can tomatoes, cut up	● Stir in flour till thoroughly blended. Add chicken broth and *undrained* tomatoes. Cook and stir till mixture is thickened and bubbly; cook and stir 1 minute more.
1 12½-ounce can tuna, drained and flaked Peanuts Snipped parsley Hot cooked rice	● Stir in tuna; heat through. Transfer to a serving bowl. Garnish with peanuts and snipped parsley. Serve over hot cooked rice. Makes 4 servings.

Do you have an appetite that can't wait more than 30 minutes for dinner? If so, satisfy that appetite with this quick and tasty dinner dish. We're betting you have all the ingredients you need right in your kitchen.

Chicken Vindaloo

Pictured on page 49.

1 **tablespoon cumin seed**	● In a blender container combine cumin seed, mustard seed, peppercorns, and fennel seed. Cover and grind till fine.
1 **tablespoon black** *or* **yellow mustard seed**	
1 **teaspoon whole black peppercorns**	
1 **teaspoon fennel seed**	

⅔ **cup vinegar**	● Add vinegar, coarsely chopped onion, garlic, coarsely chopped gingerroot, sugar, salt, turmeric, ground cinnamon, ground cloves, and ground cardamom. Cover and blend till smooth. Transfer the mixture to a bowl.
1 **medium onion, coarsely chopped**	
8 **cloves garlic**	
1 **tablespoon coarsely chopped gingerroot**	
1 **teaspoon sugar**	
1 **teaspoon salt**	
1 **teaspoon turmeric**	
1 **teaspoon ground cinnamon**	
¼ **teaspoon ground cloves**	
¼ **teaspoon ground cardamom**	

Vindaloos are curry dishes that originated with Portuguese Christians in western India. These dishes involve marinating meat or poultry in a spicy vinegar mixture and then cooking the meat in that mixture. They can be mouth-searing, but this *Chicken Vindaloo* is pleasantly spicy with a subtle heat that builds as you eat.

3 **whole medium chicken breasts, skinned, halved lengthwise, and boned**	● Cut chicken breasts crosswise into ½-inch strips. Add strips to the vinegar-spice mixture, turning to coat pieces well. Cover; chill in the refrigerator 6 hours or overnight, stirring once or twice.
1 **tablespoon cooking oil**	In a heavy saucepan heat the cooking oil over high heat. Reserving spice mixture in bowl, transfer *half* of the chicken strips to the hot oil. Cook 2 minutes, stirring frequently. Remove from saucepan. Repeat with remaining chicken, adding more oil if necessary. Remove from saucepan.
	Reduce heat to medium. Add reserved spice mixture to saucepan. Cook and stir for 1 minute.

You'll be amazed at the flavor and aroma you get by blending your own spices, the way Indian cooks do.

½ **cup water**	● Return chicken to saucepan. Add the water. Bring to boiling; reduce heat. Cover and simmer 15 minutes, stirring occasionally. Garnish with green onions, if desired. Serve with rice. Serves 6.
Hot cooked rice	

Curried Chicken Platter

1 2½- to 3-pound broiler-fryer chicken, cut up 2 tablespoons cooking oil Salt Pepper	● In a 12-inch skillet brown chicken pieces in hot oil on all sides; drain. Return chicken pieces to skillet. Sprinkle with salt and pepper.

1 cup orange juice ⅓ cup currants *or* raisins 3 tablespoons chutney, chopped 1 to 2 tablespoons curry powder ½ teaspoon ground cinnamon ½ teaspoon ground red pepper 4 medium sweet potatoes, peeled and sliced crosswise 1 inch thick	● In a bowl stir together the orange juice, currants or raisins, chopped chutney, curry powder, ground cinnamon, and ground red pepper. Add the sliced sweet potatoes to the skillet; pour orange juice mixture over chicken and sweet potatoes. Bring to boiling; reduce heat. Simmer, covered, for 30 to 40 minutes or till chicken and sweet potatoes are tender.

1 tablespoon cold water 2 teaspoons cornstarch 1 11-ounce can mandarin orange sections, drained 2 bananas, halved lengthwise and quartered ½ cup toasted slivered almonds Hot cooked rice	● Remove chicken and potatoes from skillet. Arrange on a warm platter; keep warm. Skim fat from pan juices. Measure pan juices; add water to make 1½ cups. Combine 1 tablespoon cold water and the cornstarch; add to pan juices. Cook and stir till thickened and bubbly. Cook and stir 2 minutes more. Add drained mandarin orange sections and bananas, stirring to coat. Pour fruit mixture over chicken and sweet potatoes on the platter. Garnish with toasted almonds. Serve with hot cooked rice. Makes 6 servings.

Like many popular dishes, this somewhat exotic chicken curry has cross-cultural inspiration. The fruit and sweet potatoes are courtesy of African cuisines, and the spices, chutney, currants, and almonds are India's contribution.

Curried Lamb Stroganoff with Raisin Rice

1⅓ cups water
⅔ cup long grain rice
¼ cup raisins
1 teaspoon butter *or* margarine
½ teaspoon finely shredded lemon peel
¼ teaspoon salt

● For raisin rice, in a saucepan combine water, rice, raisins, butter or margarine, lemon peel, and ¼ teaspoon salt. Bring to boiling; reduce heat. Cover and simmer 15 minutes or till rice is tender; do not lift cover. Remove from heat. Let stand, covered, about 10 minutes.

Unlike some curried dishes that are spicy hot, this one has a delicate flavor. Lemony raisin rice plays the supporting role for the starring lamb and apple feature.

2 lamb shoulder chops (about 1 pound)
1 small apple, cut into thin wedges
¼ cup chopped onion
1 clove garlic, minced
4 to 5 teaspoons curry powder
¼ teaspoon salt
¼ teaspoon ground cinnamon
2 tablespoons cooking oil

● Meanwhile, cut the meat from lamb chops into bite-size strips; discard bones.
In a 10-inch skillet cook the lamb strips, apple wedges, chopped onion, garlic, curry powder, ¼ teaspoon salt, and ground cinnamon in hot oil till meat is brown and onion is tender. Cover and cook over low heat 5 to 7 minutes more or till the meat is tender.

¼ cup plain yogurt
1 tablespoon all-purpose flour
½ cup beef broth
Parsley (optional)

● In a bowl combine yogurt and flour; stir in beef broth. Stir the yogurt mixture into the meat mixture; cook and stir till thickened and bubbly. Cook and stir 1 minute more. Serve meat mixture with the raisin rice. Garnish with parsley, if desired. Makes 3 servings.

Indian Curry Feast

In northern India, special occasions give rise to spreads such as this. One of the area's classic foods is korma, a dish in which meat is braised with yogurt or cream. Unlike some hot Indian dishes, *Beef Korma* and the other foods in this menu are gently but richly spiced.

Indians typically eat with their fingers, using bread to scoop up morsels of food. It's acceptable to use knives and forks, but purists claim the food won't taste as good.

MENU
Beef Korma
Indian Spiced Rice
Tomato-Apple Chutney
Spiced Meat Flatbread
Sautéed Cauliflower with
 Ginger
Cucumbers in Yogurt
Cool water or hot tea

MENU COUNTDOWN
6 Hours Ahead or Day Before:
Prepare Tomato-Apple Chutney; chill. Prepare Cucumbers in Yogurt; chill. Prepare Spiced Meat Flatbread; chill.
3 Hours Ahead:
Blend spice mixture and simmer meat for Beef Korma.

45 Minutes Ahead:
Cook Indian Spiced Rice. Begin cooking Sautéed Cauliflower with Ginger.
15 Minutes Ahead:
Reheat Spiced Meat Flatbread. Thicken Beef Korma with cream mixture. Finish Sautéed Cauliflower with Ginger.

Cucumbers in Yogurt
(see recipe, page 59)

Sautéed Cauliflower with Ginger *(see recipe, page 59)*

Spiced Meat Flatbread
(see recipe, page 58)

Beef Korma *(see recipe, page 56)*

Indian Spiced Rice
(see recipe, page 57)

Tomato-Apple Chutney
(see recipe, page 57)

Beef Korma

Pictured on pages 54 and 55.

1 tablespoon coriander seed 1 tablespoon cumin seed 1 teaspoon cardamom seed (without pods) 1 teaspoon crushed red pepper 6 whole cloves	● In a blender container combine coriander seed, cumin seed, cardamom seed, crushed red pepper, and whole cloves. Cover the blender container and grind the spices to a fine powder.
⅓ cup water ¼ cup slivered blanched almonds 8 cloves garlic 1 tablespoon coarsely chopped gingerroot 1½ teaspoons salt ½ teaspoon ground cinnamon	● Add ⅓ cup water, the slivered blanched almonds, garlic cloves, coarsely chopped gingerroot, salt, and ground cinnamon. Cover the blender container and blend till the mixture has a paste consistency.
2 pounds beef *or* lamb stew meat, cut into 1-inch cubes 1 tablespoon cooking oil	● In a 4-quart saucepan or Dutch oven brown *half* of the meat on all sides in 1 tablespoon hot oil; remove. Repeat with remaining meat, adding 1 tablespoon additional oil if needed; remove.
2 tablespoons cooking oil 2 medium onions, thinly sliced and separated into rings	● Heat 2 tablespoons oil in the saucepan; add onions. Cook and stir over medium-high heat for 8 to 10 minutes or till onions begin to brown. Reduce heat to medium. Add blended spice mixture; cook and stir 3 to 4 minutes more or till slightly browned.
½ cup water	● Add meat and ½ cup water to the saucepan. Cover and simmer for 1½ to 1¾ hours or till meat is tender; stir occasionally.
¾ cup whipping cream ½ cup plain yogurt 2 tablespoons all-purpose flour ¼ teaspoon Homemade Garam Masala (see recipe, page 92) *or* garam masala 2 tablespoons snipped coriander *or* parsley Indian Spiced Rice (see recipe, page 57) *or* hot cooked rice	● Stir together whipping cream, yogurt, flour, and garam masala. Stir mixture into Dutch oven; cook and stir till thickened and bubbly. Cook and stir 1 to 2 minutes more. Transfer to a serving bowl; sprinkle with coriander or parsley. Serve with Indian Spiced Rice or hot cooked rice. Makes 8 servings.

One of the classic recipes of northern India is the *korma.* **Rich with yogurt, cream, and aromatic spices, it typically is served on special occasions. The name actually means "braise" and describes the method in which the blended spices in liquid penetrate the meat.**

Indian Spiced Rice

Pictured on page 55.

¼ cup sliced green onion
2 tablespoons butter *or* margarine

● In a saucepan cook green onion in butter or margarine till onion is tender but not brown.

1⅓ cups long grain rice
½ teaspoon salt
½ teaspoon Homemade Garam Masala (see recipe, page 92) *or* garam masala
⅛ teaspoon ground red pepper
1 small clove garlic, minced
2⅔ cups water

● Stir in rice, salt, garam masala, ground red pepper, and garlic. Cook and stir over medium heat for 1 minute.
   Add water. Bring to boiling; reduce heat. Cover and simmer for 15 minutes; do not lift lid. Remove saucepan from heat. Let stand, covered, for 10 minutes. Makes 8 servings.

An Indian meal rarely is eaten without rice. Not only does it soak up the liquids of the other dishes, rice acts as a buffer for spicier dishes in the meal. Serve saucy *Beef Korma* over part but not all of this delicately seasoned rice, leaving some rice to eat with the rest of the meal.

Tomato-Apple Chutney

Pictured on page 55.

2 large ripe tomatoes, finely chopped (2 cups)
2 large cooking apples, finely chopped (2 cups)
1 cup packed brown sugar
¾ cup red wine vinegar
1 medium onion, finely chopped (½ cup)
½ cup water
¼ cup light raisins
½ teaspoon salt
¼ teaspoon ground red pepper
1 tablespoon mixed pickling spice
2 inches stick cinnamon, broken in half

● In a saucepan combine chopped tomatoes, chopped apples, brown sugar, red wine vinegar, chopped onion, water, raisins, salt, and ground red pepper. Tie pickling spice and stick cinnamon in several thicknesses of cheesecloth to make a bag. Add to tomato mixture. Bring to boiling; reduce heat. Simmer, uncovered, about 45 minutes or till mixture is thickened, stirring frequently.
   Remove and discard spice bag. Transfer chutney to a bowl. Cover and chill. Store in the refrigerator up to 4 weeks or freeze. Makes 2½ cups.

Excite and refresh your palate by taking intermittent bites of this tangy fruit mixture with spicier foods.
   To make it easier to remove the whole spices from the chutney after cooking, tie them together in a spice bag made from several layers of cheesecloth.

Spiced Meat Flatbread

Pictured on page 55.

1¼ cups whole wheat flour
¾ cup all-purpose flour
2 tablespoons shortening
⅔ cup warm water
   (100° to 110°)

● In a mixing bowl combine whole wheat flour and all-purpose flour; cut in shortening till crumbly. Add *half* of the water all at once; mix in with a fork. Gradually mix in remaining water, 1 tablespoon at a time, till dough forms a ball and can be kneaded.
   On a lightly floured surface, knead dough about 10 minutes or till smooth and elastic. Cover; let rest 15 minutes.

Flatten each portion of dough into a 4½-inch circle. Center 1 rounded tablespoon filling on each.

½ pound bulk Italian
   sausage
½ cup chopped onion
1 clove garlic, minced
1 teaspoon ground cumin
¼ teaspoon salt

● For filling, in a skillet cook sausage, onion, and garlic till meat is brown, stirring to break meat into small pieces; drain. Stir in cumin and salt. Remove from heat. Cool completely.

● Divide dough into 8 equal portions. On a lightly floured surface flatten one dough portion with your hand or roll out into a 4½-inch circle. Keep remaining dough covered. Place *1 rounded tablespoon* of filling in center of dough, as shown at top. Bring up edges of dough to enclose filling completely, as shown at center. Pinch to seal. Repeat with remaining portions of dough.

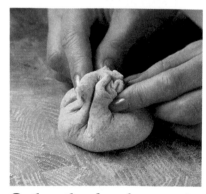

Gather the dough up and around the filling, pinching the seam to seal.

● Gently roll out each ball of dough into a 6-inch circle so filling spreads evenly inside dough, as shown at bottom. Dust occasionally with flour to prevent sticking to surface.

● Heat a griddle or skillet over medium heat about 2 minutes or till hot. Place one circle on griddle; cook about 2 minutes or till brown spots appear. Turn; cook 30 to 60 seconds more. Cool on a wire rack. Repeat with remaining. To store, wrap each in foil and refrigerate. (Or, wrap in moisture- and vaporproof wrap and freeze.) Makes 8 servings.
   Note: To reheat, rewrap each flatbread in foil, if frozen. Warm refrigerated or frozen flatbread in a 300° oven about 15 minutes or till heated through.

Roll out again, this time into a 6-inch circle.

Sautéed Cauliflower with Ginger

Pictured on page 54.

2 tablespoons cooking oil ½ teaspoon fennel seed	● In a 12-inch skillet heat oil over medium-high heat. Add fennel seed; heat and stir for 30 to 60 seconds or till seed turns brown. Remove from heat.
4 teaspoons grated gingerroot ½ teaspoon salt ¼ teaspoon turmeric ¼ teaspoon ground red pepper 1 large head cauliflower, broken into small flowerets (6 cups) ¼ cup water	● Stir the grated gingerroot, salt, turmeric, and ground red pepper into the oil and fennel seed in the skillet. Add cauliflower flowerets and water. Bring to boiling; reduce heat. Cover and cook for 10 to 12 minutes or till the cauliflower is crisp-tender, stirring occasionally.
½ cup coarsely chopped cashews 2 teaspoons lemon juice 2 tablespoons snipped parsley *or* coriander	● Increase heat to medium. Uncover and stir-fry 3 to 4 minutes or till liquid is evaporated. Stir in cashews and lemon juice. Sprinkle with parsley or coriander. Makes 8 servings.

Indian cooks use fresh gingerroot to accent the flavors of their vegetable dishes. You'll need about 2 inches of gingerroot that's ¾ inch in diameter for this recipe because each inch of the root will yield about 2 teaspoons grated.

Cucumbers in Yogurt

Pictured on page 54.

2 medium cucumbers, peeled and finely shredded 1 8-ounce carton plain yogurt 2 tablespoons chopped fresh mint *or* snipped parsley ¼ teaspoon salt	● In a bowl combine the finely shredded cucumbers, plain yogurt, chopped mint or snipped parsley, and salt. Cover and chill in the refrigerator. Makes 8 servings.

Yogurt is included in almost every Indian meal, by itself, in a sauce, or with vegetables. Mixed with cool cucumbers and fresh mint, the yogurt in this side dish gives your taste buds a rest, especially if you are unaccustomed to so much flavor in one meal.

Twice-Cooked Noodles with Pork

1 **pound boneless pork**	● Partially freeze pork; thinly slice into bite-size strips.
6 **ounces fine noodles** *or* **spaghetti**	● In a saucepan cook noodles according to package directions. Rinse in cold water and drain well.
1 **medium cucumber, halved lengthwise and seeded** 3 **tablespoons soy sauce** 2 **teaspoons cornstarch** ⅓ **cup water** 1 **tablespoon catsup** 1 **teaspoon sugar**	● Meanwhile, cut halved cucumber crosswise into thin slices; set aside. In a bowl stir soy sauce into cornstarch; stir in water, catsup, and sugar. Set aside.
3 **to 4 tablespoons cooking oil**	● In a large skillet or wok heat *2 tablespoons* cooking oil over medium heat. Add *half* of the cooked noodles. Cook and stir 7 to 9 minutes or till slightly crisp. Transfer to a plate. Repeat with remaining 1 to 2 tablespoons cooking oil and the remaining noodles.
2 **tablespoons Red Pepper Oil (see recipe, page 92) *or* chili oil** 2 **cloves garlic, minced** 1 **teaspoon grated gingerroot**	● In the skillet or wok heat *1 tablespoon* Red Pepper Oil or chili oil. Add garlic and gingerroot; stir-fry 30 seconds. Add cucumber; stir-fry 30 seconds. Remove cucumber, leaving any oil in the skillet. Add remaining 1 tablespoon Red Pepper Oil or chili oil to skillet; add pork and stir-fry 2 to 3 minutes or till brown. Stir the cornstarch mixture; stir into pork in skillet. Cook and stir till thickened and bubbly; cook and stir 2 minutes more. Stir in cucumber and noodles; heat through. Makes 4 servings.

Noodles in a stir-fry dish? The Chinese have been doing it for years. To use noodles in a stir-fry such as this one, cook the noodles in water first, then stir-fry them till slightly crisp. Add them to the other stir-fried ingredients at the end.

The mouth-tingling heat in this dish comes from chili oil. This pungent seasoning is sesame oil that has been infused with fiery crushed red pepper. Buy it in an Oriental market or make your own using the recipe for Red Pepper Oil on page 92.

Spaghetti with Meat Sauce

1 pound bulk Italian
   sausage
½ cup chopped onion
½ cup chopped green
   pepper
1 clove garlic, minced

● For sauce, in a large saucepan or Dutch oven cook sausage, onion, green pepper, and garlic till meat is brown and vegetables are tender. Drain off fat.

1 28-ounce can tomatoes,
   cut up
1 8-ounce can tomato sauce
¼ cup water
2 teaspoons dried oregano,
   crushed
2 teaspoons dried basil,
   crushed
1 teaspoon sugar
¾ teaspoon dried thyme,
   crushed
½ teaspoon salt
½ teaspoon ground allspice
¼ teaspoon crushed red
   pepper
1 bay leaf

● Stir in the *undrained* cut-up tomatoes, tomato sauce, water, dried oregano, dried basil, sugar, dried thyme, salt, ground allspice, crushed red pepper, and bay leaf.
   Bring the mixture to boiling; reduce heat. Simmer, uncovered, for 30 to 40 minutes or till the sauce is the desired consistency, stirring occasionally. Remove the bay leaf from the sauce.

8 ounces spaghetti
   Grated Parmesan cheese
   (optional)

● Meanwhile, cook spaghetti according to package directions; drain. Serve sauce over spaghetti. If desired, pass grated Parmesan cheese. Makes 4 servings.

If you like your spaghetti sauce nice and spicy with lots of meat, here's your recipe. The hotter the Italian sausage you use, the wilder the sauce.

Layered Mostaccioli

4 ounces mostaccioli	● Cook mostaccioli in a large amount of boiling salted water about 14 minutes or just till tender; drain.
1 pound ground beef, pork, *or* lamb ¼ cup chopped onion ¼ cup chopped green pepper 1 clove garlic, minced	● Meanwhile, in a large saucepan cook ground meat, onion, green pepper, and garlic till meat is brown and vegetables are tender. Drain off fat.
1 16-ounce can tomatoes, cut up 1 6-ounce can tomato paste ½ cup water 1 tablespoon chili powder 1 teaspoon crushed red pepper ½ teaspoon salt ½ teaspoon dried oregano, crushed ½ teaspoon ground cinnamon ¼ teaspoon sugar ⅛ teaspoon black pepper	● Stir in *undrained* tomatoes, tomato paste, water, chili powder, crushed red pepper, salt, dried oregano, ground cinnamon, sugar, and black pepper. Bring the meat mixture to boiling; reduce heat. Cover the saucepan and simmer for 30 minutes, stirring occasionally.
1 slightly beaten egg 1½ cups ricotta *or* cream-style cottage cheese ½ cup grated Parmesan cheese	● Stir together beaten egg and ricotta cheese. Stir mostaccioli into meat mixture. Transfer *half* of the mostaccioli mixture to a 12x7½x2-inch baking dish. Spread with cheese mixture. Top with the remaining mostaccioli mixture. Sprinkle with Parmesan cheese.
Sliced pitted ripe olives (optional)	● Cover and bake in a 350° oven about 30 minutes or till heated through. Let stand 10 minutes before serving If desired, garnish with sliced ripe olives. Makes 6 to 8 servings.

Mostaccioli or "little moustaches" are tube-shaped noodles with slanted ends that allow sauce to seep inside each piece. Together with a uniquely spiced meat sauce, they form the top and bottom layers of this lasagna-like dish. The layer in the middle? Cheese, of course!

Bratwurst-and-Beer-Sauced Pasta

¾ pound fully cooked bratwurst *or* Polish sausage	● Cut the bratwurst or Polish sausage into ½-inch slices. In a skillet cook the sausage slices till brown. Remove sausage and drain on paper towels. Drain fat from skillet.
¼ cup sliced green onion 3 tablespoons butter *or* margarine 3 tablespoons all-purpose flour 1 teaspoon dry mustard 1 teaspoon caraway seed ½ to ¾ teaspoon ground red pepper ⅛ teaspoon salt	● In the same skillet cook the ¼ cup sliced green onion in butter or margarine till tender but not brown. Stir in the flour, dry mustard, caraway seed, ground red pepper, and salt till thoroughly combined.
1 cup milk 1½ cups shredded American cheese (6 ounces) ¾ cup shredded Swiss cheese (3 ounces) ⅔ cup beer	● Add milk all at once. Cook and stir till mixture is thickened and bubbly. Cook and stir 1 minute more. Stir in the shredded American cheese, shredded Swiss cheese, and beer, stirring till cheeses are melted. Add browned sausage; heat through.
1 10-ounce package spaetzle *or* 6 ounces medium noodles, cooked according to package directions 1 tablespoon sliced green onion (optional)	● Serve the sausage mixture over cooked spaetzle or noodles. Garnish with additional sliced green onion, if desired. Makes 6 servings.

This pasta dish is generous on German gusto. Plump bratwurst, two kinds of cheese, beer, and caraway seed go into a wonderfully creamy sauce to top spaetzle or noodles. Ground red pepper and dry mustard give it an unexpected spicy kick.

Southwestern Chicken-and-Pasta Salad

4 ounces medium shell, elbow, *or* corkscrew macaroni	● Cook macaroni in a large amount of boiling salted water till tender but firm (10 to 12 minutes for shell or elbow macaroni and about 8 minutes for corkscrew macaroni). Drain. Rinse with cold water; drain.
¼ cup salad oil 2 tablespoons white wine vinegar 1 tablespoon lime juice ½ teaspoon chili powder ¼ teaspoon salt ¼ teaspoon dry mustard Several drops bottled hot pepper sauce	● For dressing, in a screw-top jar combine salad oil, white wine vinegar, lime juice, chili powder, salt, dry mustard, and hot pepper sauce. Cover and shake well. Pour over drained macaroni, stirring to coat evenly.
3 fresh *or* canned jalapeño *or* serrano peppers	● See instructions on page 6 for handling and preparing fresh chili peppers. Broil and peel fresh peppers; remove stem ends and seeds. (Or, rinse and seed canned peppers.) Chop the peppers. Add to the pasta mixture.
1 cup chopped cooked chicken 1 8¾-ounce can whole kernel corn, drained ½ medium avocado, seeded, peeled, and cut into bite-size chunks 2 ounces Monterey Jack cheese *or* Monterey Jack cheese with jalapeño peppers, cubed ¼ cup sliced pitted ripe olives 2 tablespoons sliced green onion 1 2-ounce jar diced pimiento, drained Lettuce leaves	● Stir in chicken, corn, avocado chunks, cheese cubes, sliced olives, sliced green onion, and pimiento. Cover and chill for several hours or overnight. Serve on lettuce-lined plates. Makes 4 servings.

Even though this pasta salad is served cold, the jalapeños will make your mouth hot. If that makes you a little leery, use the canned jalapeño peppers, which usually are milder than the fresh. On the other hand, if you want even more of a burning sensation, use the serrano peppers which are hotter, and leave the fleshy ribs and the seeds in the peppers.

Thai Beef with Broccoli

1 **pound beef top round steak**	● Partially freeze the round steak; with a sharp knife slice the meat very thinly into bite-size strips.	**The Thai people are known for their fiery foods, mainly because they use hot peppers with reckless abandon. To put out the fire, they serve plenty of rice, and as a beverage, iced weak tea or iced water. Though we've tempered the fire in this recipe to please Western palates, you might want to take some of the same fire-fighting precautions.**
¼ **cup water**		
4 **cloves garlic**	In a blender container combine water, garlic, 2 tablespoons cooking oil, lemon juice, soy sauce, crushed red pepper, cornstarch, and nam pla. Cover the blender container and blend till smooth. Set aside.	
2 **tablespoons cooking oil**		
2 **tablespoons lemon juice**		
2 **tablespoons soy sauce**		
1½ **to 2 teaspoons crushed red pepper**		
1½ **teaspoons cornstarch**		
1 **to 1½ teaspoons nam pla (fish sauce)**		

2 **tablespoons cooking oil**	● Heat a wok or large skillet over high heat; add 2 tablespoons cooking oil. Stir-fry broccoli 3 to 4 minutes or till crisp-tender. Remove from wok.	**Nam pla is a dark-colored fish sauce that resembles soy sauce in appearance and saltiness. It is an essential flavoring ingredient in Thai cooking. You'll find it at Oriental markets, perhaps under its Vietnamese name of nuoc mam.**
4 **cups broccoli cut into 1-inch pieces**		
	Add more oil if necessary. Add *half* of the beef strips; stir-fry 2 to 3 minutes or till brown. Remove beef. Stir-fry remaining beef 2 to 3 minutes. Return all beef and broccoli to skillet.	

Deep-Fried Wonton Strips *or* **hot cooked rice**	● Stir in the cornstarch mixture. Cook and stir till thickened and bubbly. Cover and cook 1 minute more. Serve with Deep-Fried Wonton Strips or rice. Makes 4 servings.

Deep-Fried Wonton Strips: Cut ¼ pound *egg roll skins or wonton skins* into 2x1-inch strips. Fry strips, a few at a time, in deep hot *cooking oil* (375°) about 10 seconds per side or just till strips are golden. Remove; drain on paper towels. Keep warm in oven.

Peppery Beef with Rice Noodles
(see recipe, page 68)

Thai Beef with Broccoli

**Many-Flavored Chicken
and Vegetables**
(see recipe, page 69)

Peppery Beef with Rice Noodles

Pictured on page 67.

1 pound beef flank steak	● Partially freeze beef; slice with the grain into ⅛-inch-thick strips. Slice across the grain into 2-inch-long strips.
½ cup water 3 tablespoons soy sauce 2 tablespoons sake *or* dry sherry 1 teaspoon sugar ½ teaspoon grated gingerroot	● For marinade, in a bowl combine water, soy sauce, sake or sherry, sugar, and gingerroot. Stir in the beef. Let stand at room temperature 30 minutes.
2 ounces rice sticks Cooking oil for deep-fat frying	● Meanwhile, fry unsoaked rice sticks in deep hot cooking oil (375°) about 5 seconds or just till sticks puff and rise to the top. Remove; drain on paper towels. Crush rice sticks slightly; set aside.
2 tablespoons cooking oil 1 cup julienne-cut celery 1 cup thinly sliced carrots* ½ medium green pepper, cut into julienne strips 1½ to 2 teaspoons crushed red pepper	● In a wok or large skillet heat 2 tablespoons cooking oil. Stir-fry celery, carrots, and green pepper for 4 minutes. Remove from wok. If necessary add additional oil to the wok. Drain beef, reserving marinade. Add *half* of the beef and *half* of the crushed red pepper to the wok; stir-fry 3 minutes or till meat is brown. Remove from wok. Repeat with the remaining beef and crushed red pepper. Remove.
1½ teaspoons cornstarch 2 teaspoons sesame oil	● Combine cornstarch and reserved marinade; add to wok. Cook and stir till thickened and bubbly; cook and stir 2 minutes more. Add the meat, vegetables, and sesame oil; cook and stir about 1 minute or till mixture is heated through. Remove from heat. Serve the rice sticks with the beef mixture. Makes 4 servings. ***Note:** To make sliced carrot flowers, use a punch-type can opener to score the unsliced carrots lengthwise, making five or six grooves; slice crosswise.

Our panel of hot food fanatics labeled this dish "warm," telling us that the first bite was not hot, but the heat increased as they ate. One panel member added, "The crunchy texture of the rice sticks is a nice counterpoint to the beef."

When you fry rice sticks, they puff instantly, making a spectacular show. Fry a few at a time in deep hot cooking oil (375°) about 5 seconds or just till the sticks puff and rise to the top. Lift out with a strainer and drain on paper towels.

Many-Flavored Chicken and Vegetables

Pictured on page 67.

2 **whole medium chicken breasts**	● Remove and discard the skin from chicken breasts. Halve breasts lengthwise; remove and discard bones. Cut chicken into 1-inch pieces.
3 **tablespoons soy sauce** ½ **teaspoon Homemade Five-Spice Powder (see recipe, page 93) *or* five-spice powder**	● In a bowl combine soy sauce and five-spice powder; stir in chicken pieces. Let stand at room temperature 15 minutes.
3 **tablespoons sugar** 2 **teaspoons cornstarch** 3 **tablespoons water** 3 **tablespoons white vinegar**	● Stir together sugar and cornstarch; stir in water and vinegar. Set aside.
2 **tablespoons cooking oil** 2 **dried hot peppers, seeded and finely chopped** 1 **teaspoon grated gingerroot**	● In a wok or large skillet heat oil. Add chopped peppers; stir-fry 2 minutes. Add gingerroot; stir-fry 30 seconds more.
1 **medium sweet potato, peeled and cut into julienne strips** 8 **fresh medium mushrooms, sliced (1 cup)** 4 **green onions, cut into 1-inch pieces (⅓ cup)** **Green onion brush (see hint at far right)**	● Add sweet potato strips, sliced mushrooms, and cut-up green onions. Stir-fry 3 to 4 minutes or just till tender; remove from wok. If necessary, add additional oil. Add *half* of the *undrained* chicken mixture to the wok; stir-fry 2 minutes. Remove. Stir-fry remaining chicken mixture 2 minutes. Return all chicken mixture to wok. Stir cornstarch mixture and stir into chicken. Cook and stir till thickened and bubbly. Cook and stir 1 minute more. Stir in vegetables. Cover and cook 1 minute. Garnish with green onion brush. Makes 4 servings.

Sweet, sour, fragrant, and mildly hot describe this delightful Chinese chicken dish. To achieve the right heat, use the dried hot peppers found in Oriental markets or those on your supermarket spice shelf. Five-spice powder, a Chinese seasoning that is more aromatic than spicy hot, can be made at home using the recipe on page 93, or purchased at Oriental markets and some supermarkets.

To make a green onion brush for a garnish, trim a green onion at both ends. Cut thin 2-inch slits at one or both ends. Place in ice water to crisp and curl the ends.

Szechuan Chicken with Peanuts

2 **whole medium chicken breasts**	● Remove and discard the skin from chicken breasts. Halve breasts lengthwise; remove and discard bones. Cut chicken into 1-inch pieces.
1 **egg white** 1 **tablespoon cornstarch** 1 **teaspoon dry sherry** 1 **teaspoon sesame oil (optional)** ½ **teaspoon sugar**	● In a bowl combine egg white; 1 tablespoon cornstarch; the dry sherry; sesame oil, if desired; and sugar. Add chicken pieces; with your hands, work the cornstarch mixture into the chicken. Set aside.
⅓ **cup cold water** 2 **tablespoons soy sauce** 1 **teaspoon cornstarch**	● In a small bowl stir cold water and soy sauce into the 1 teaspoon cornstarch. Set aside.
3 **tablespoons cooking oil** 6 **dried hot peppers, quartered, _or_** 1 **tablespoon crushed red pepper** 4 **cloves garlic, minced** 2 **teaspoons grated gingerroot**	● Heat a wok or large skillet over high heat; add cooking oil. Stir-fry dried hot peppers or crushed red pepper, garlic, and gingerroot for 30 seconds. Add chicken pieces; stir-fry 1 minute.
½ **cup dry roasted peanuts** 1 **6-ounce package frozen pea pods, thawed** **Hot cooked rice**	● Stir cornstarch mixture; stir into wok or skillet. Cook and stir till thickened and bubbly; cook and stir 2 minutes more or till mixture coats chicken. Stir in peanuts and pea pods; heat through. Serve with hot cooked rice. Makes 4 servings.

This dish is considered a classic in Szechuan cooking, a lively cuisine of southwestern China. The mixture of chicken, pea pods, and peanuts is coated with a thin glaze instead of a sauce and is best served with rice, rather than over it.

Dried hot peppers are what make this and other Szechuan dishes red-hot. These thin, fingerlike red peppers usually are sold in cellophane bags in Oriental, Italian, and Spanish markets. If you can't get the whole dried peppers, substitute crushed red pepper.

Pork with Pine Nuts

1 **pound boneless pork** 1 **egg white** 1 **tablespoon sake** *or* **dry sherry** ½ **teaspoon sugar**	● Cut pork into julienne strips about 2x¼x¼ inches. Combine egg white, sake or dry sherry, and sugar. Add pork and stir till thoroughly mixed. Set aside.
1 **teaspoon cornstarch** ½ **teaspoon salt** 2 **tablespoons chicken broth**	● Stir together cornstarch and salt; stir in chicken broth. Set aside.
2 **tablespoons cooking oil** 3 *or* **4 fresh jalapeño** *or* **serrano peppers, seeded and cut into julienne strips (¼ cup)** 1 **teaspoon grated gingerroot** 1 **teaspoon crushed red pepper**	● In a well-seasoned or nonstick wok or large skillet heat *1 tablespoon* of the cooking oil. Add jalapeño or serrano peppers and stir-fry 1 minute; remove peppers. Add *half* of the pork mixture. Stir-fry 2 to 3 minutes. Remove. Heat remaining oil; add gingerroot and crushed red pepper. Add remaining pork mixture and stir-fry 2 to 3 minutes.
¼ **cup toasted pine nuts** *or* **sliced almonds** 8 **Boston lettuce leaves**	● Return chili peppers and all pork to wok; stir cornstarch mixture and add to wok. Cook and stir 1 minute. Stir in pine nuts or almonds. To serve, spoon about *⅓ cup* of the pork mixture onto each lettuce leaf near one edge. Fold edge nearest filling up and over filling. Fold in the two sides envelope-fashion, then roll up. (Or, serve the pork mixture in open lettuce leaves.) Makes 4 servings.

Bundle up strips of pork, fresh chili peppers, and pine nuts in tender lettuce leaves for a popular Oriental presentation of this mildly spicy dish. Or, serve the pork mixture "open-face" in the lettuce leaves. Consider Chinese vegetables and hot rice as side dishes to complete the meal.

Sausage and Pineapple Pizza

½ pound bulk chorizo *or* Italian sausage	● In a skillet brown the sausage; drain off fat. Set sausage aside.
1 package active dry yeast ½ cup warm water (110° to 115°) 2½ cups packaged biscuit mix	● In a bowl soften yeast in warm water; add biscuit mix. Mix well. Turn out onto a lightly floured surface; knead 25 strokes. Cover; let rest 10 minutes.
1 15-ounce can tomato sauce 2 *or* 3 jalapeño peppers, rinsed, seeded, and chopped (about ¼ cup) 1 teaspoon dried oregano, crushed ½ teaspoon ground cumin Cornmeal (optional)	● Meanwhile, stir together tomato sauce, jalapeño peppers, oregano, and cumin. Grease a 15x10x1-inch baking pan. If desired, sprinkle lightly with cornmeal. Pat or roll out dough onto the bottom and up the sides of the prepared pan. Bake in a 425° oven for 8 to 10 minutes or till light brown.
1 8¼-ounce can crushed pineapple, well drained 1 medium green pepper, cut into strips 1½ cups shredded mozzarella cheese (6 ounces) ¼ cup grated Parmesan cheese	● Spread tomato sauce mixture over baked crust. Top with cooked sausage, crushed pineapple, and green pepper strips. Sprinkle mozzarella and Parmesan cheeses atop. Bake in the 425° oven for 10 to 15 minutes or till bubbly. Makes 6 servings.

The dough for the light crispy crust is so easy to work with, you can pat it into the pan with your hands. Form the dough to the pan so that it extends up the sides.

Gunpowder Pork Chops

2 teaspoons ground white pepper 2 teaspoons ground red pepper 2 teaspoons ground black pepper 6 pork chops, cut 1 inch thick	● In a bowl combine white pepper, red pepper, and black pepper. Rub the surfaces of *eqch* chop with about *1 teaspoon* of the pepper mixture, distributing evenly.
Bottled picante sauce (optional)	● Place chops on the rack of an unheated broiler pan. Broil 3 to 4 inches from heat for 20 to 25 minutes total or till done, turning once. If desired, serve with picante sauce. Makes 6 servings.

The three-pepper "gunpowder" on these loaded chops put them on our extra-hot list and prompted one spicy food fanatic to call them "a real nose runner." If you're lookin' for double trouble, serve them with *hot* picante sauce.

Tex-Mex Macaroni and Cheese

¾ cup elbow macaroni	● Cook the macaroni in a large amount of boiling salted water about 10 minutes or just till tender; drain.
1 pound bulk chorizo *or* Italian sausage ½ cup chopped onion 1 clove garlic, minced	● In a large skillet cook sausage, onion, and garlic till sausage is brown and onion is tender; drain off fat.
1 10¾-ounce can condensed cheddar cheese soup ½ cup dairy sour cream ½ cup milk 1 4-ounce can diced green chili peppers, drained	● In a mixing bowl stir together cheddar cheese soup, sour cream, milk, and drained chili peppers; stir in the cooked macaroni and the sausage mixture. Transfer to a 2-quart casserole.
2 cups tortilla chips, crushed to ¾ cup	● Sprinkle crushed tortilla chips over mixture. Bake, uncovered, in a 350° oven for 30 to 35 minutes or till heated through. Makes 4 servings.

Determine the spiciness of this meaty mac 'n' cheese dish by the kind of sausage you use. Chorizo is quite hot, and Italian sausage comes in varying degrees of spiciness. For a milder seasoning level, use bulk pork sausage instead.

Conquistador Quiche

1 9-inch frozen unbaked deep-dish pastry shell	● Thaw the frozen pastry shell for 10 minutes at room temperature. If desired, transfer to a 9-inch pie plate. Do not prick the pastry shell. Bake in a 450° oven for 5 minutes. Cool on a wire rack. Reduce oven temperature to 325°.	Brave the jalapeño peppers and spicy-hot sausage of this hearty quiche and you will have conquered a world of flavorful eating. Top your serving the way you like it—with shredded lettuce, sour cream, tomatoes, or all three.
½ pound bulk chorizo *or* Italian sausage ¼ cup chopped onion 1 clove garlic, minced	● In a skillet cook chorizo or Italian sausage, onion, and garlic over medium-high heat till sausage is brown and onion is tender; drain off fat. Blot the sausage with paper towels to absorb remaining fat. Set aside.	
1 cup shredded Monterey Jack *or* cheddar cheese *or* a combination (4 ounces) 2 pickled jalapeño peppers, rinsed, seeded, and chopped (3 tablespoons)	● In the partially baked pastry shell layer the shredded cheese, the seeded and chopped jalapeño peppers, and the sausage mixture.	
3 beaten eggs 1½ cups milk ¼ teaspoon salt	● Combine eggs, milk, and salt; pour over sausage in pastry. Bake in the 325° oven about 50 minutes or till a knife inserted near center comes out clean.	
Shredded lettuce Dairy sour cream Cherry tomatoes, cut into wedges	● Let the quiche stand 10 minutes before serving. To serve, top individual servings with lettuce, sour cream, and tomato wedges. Makes 6 servings.	

Chicken-Potato Volcanoes

2 large baking potatoes (7 to 8 ounces each)	● Scrub potatoes. Prick potatoes with a fork. Bake in a 425° oven for 40 to 60 minutes or till done. Cut a thin slice from the top of each potato. Scoop out the pulp, being careful not to tear the shells, and leaving ¼-inch walls, as shown. Place the potato pulp in a bowl and break up large chunks; set aside.
1 tablespoon butter *or* margarine **1 tablespoon all-purpose flour** **½ cup milk** **½ cup shredded American cheese with jalapeño peppers (2 ounces)**	● Meanwhile, for cheese sauce, in a small saucepan melt 1 tablespoon butter or margarine. Stir in flour. Add milk all at once. Cook and stir till the mixture is thickened and bubbly; cook and stir 1 minute more. Stir in shredded cheese. Cook and stir till cheese is melted and sauce is smooth.
1 tablespoon chopped onion **1 tablespoon butter *or* margarine** **2 tablespoons chopped pimiento** **1 tablespoon chopped fresh anaheim peppers *or* diced canned green chili peppers** **1 tablespoon chopped fresh hot yellow chili peppers** **½ teaspoon dried oregano, crushed** **¼ teaspoon ground cumin** **¼ teaspoon salt**	● In a medium skillet cook the chopped onion in 1 tablespoon butter or margarine till the onion is tender but not brown. Add the chopped pimiento, chopped fresh anaheim or diced canned green chili peppers, chopped fresh hot yellow chili peppers, dried oregano, ground cumin, and salt. Cook the chili pepper mixture over medium heat for 1 minute, stirring constantly.
¾ cup chopped cooked chicken	● Add chicken, reserved potato pulp, and ¼ *cup* of the cheese sauce to the chili pepper mixture; heat through. Heap into the potato shells. Top with the remaining sauce. Makes 2 servings.

Cut a thin slice from each potato and carefully scoop out the pulp with a grapefruit knife or spoon, leaving the shell intact.

Then make mouth-watering mountains by filling the hollowed-out potato shells with a spicy chicken mixture. Lavish them with a slightly volatile jalapeño-cheese sauce and get ready for an explosion of flavor.

Forty-Clove Garlic Chicken

1	2½- to 3-pound broiler-fryer chicken, cut up Salt	
2	tablespoons cooking oil	

● Sprinkle the chicken pieces lightly with salt. In a 12-inch skillet cook the chicken pieces on all sides in hot cooking oil about 15 minutes or till brown. Arrange the chicken pieces in a 12x7½x2-inch baking dish.

40	cloves unpeeled garlic
½	cup dry white wine
1	small lemon, quartered Several dashes ground red pepper

● Add *unpeeled* garlic cloves and wine to the baking dish. Squeeze lemon quarters over the chicken, adding the squeezed quarters to the baking dish. Lightly sprinkle the ground red pepper over the chicken. Cover and bake in a 325° oven about 1 hour or till the chicken pieces are tender.

● Transfer the chicken pieces and garlic cloves to a serving platter. Discard lemon quarters. Spoon the cooking liquid over the chicken pieces. Makes 6 servings.

Note: To eat a garlic clove, squeeze the unpeeled clove between your thumb and index finger till the clove pops out of its peel into your mouth.

After eating a dish made with 40 cloves of garlic, you might think you should restrict yourself to solitary confinement. But relax. Because the garlic cloves are cooked whole instead of minced, they retain most of their flavor, contributing only a hint of garlic taste to the surrounding food. The garlic cloves themselves mellow enough during cooking that you can eat them whole.

The number of cloves in a garlic bulb varies, but we used three whole bulbs in order to get the 40 cloves we needed.

Steak au Poivre

2 to 4 teaspoons whole black peppercorns *or* 1 to 2 teaspoons cracked black pepper 4 beef top loin steaks, cut 1 inch thick (about 2 pounds)	● If using whole black peppercorns, use a mortar and pestle to coarsely crack the peppercorns. Slash the fat edge of the steaks at 1-inch intervals. Sprinkle one side of each steak with ⅛ to ¼ *teaspoon* of the cracked peppercorns or cracked black pepper; rub over meat, pressing into the surface. Repeat on other side of steaks.
2 tablespoons butter *or* margarine Salt	● In a 12-inch skillet melt butter or margarine. Add steaks; cook over medium-high heat to desired doneness, turning once. (Allow 12 to 14 minutes total cooking time for medium doneness.) Sprinkle with salt.
¼ cup brandy	● Pour brandy over steaks in the skillet. Light a long match and carefully ignite the brandy. Allow flames to subside.
¼ cup water 1 tablespoon Dijon-style mustard ½ teaspoon instant beef bouillon granules Fresh mushrooms	● Transfer steaks to a warm platter. Stir water, Dijon-style mustard, and instant beef bouillon granules into brandy in skillet. Bring to boiling; pour over steaks. Garnish with fresh mushrooms, if desired. Makes 4 servings.

Poivre, the French word for pepper, is the predominant seasoning in this *flambéed* or flamed classic. To be sure it will flame, use a brandy that's at least 70 proof.

Indian Spiced Burgers

1	slightly beaten egg
2	tablespoons sliced green onion
2	tablespoons fine dry bread crumbs
2	teaspoons curry powder
1	teaspoon prepared mustard
¼	teaspoon crushed red pepper
¼	teaspoon salt
½	pound lean ground beef

● In a mixing bowl combine egg, onion, bread crumbs, curry powder, 1 teaspoon mustard, the red pepper, and salt. Add ground meat; mix well. Shape into two ½-inch-thick patties. Cut the patties in half crosswise.

In a skillet cook patty halves over medium-high heat about 8 minutes, turning once. (Or, place on the unheated rack of a broiler pan; broil 5 inches from heat about 10 minutes, turning once.)

Looking for a way to spice up plain hamburgers? Do it Indian-style by adding curry powder to the ground beef mixture. Then, serve the burgers in pita bread instead of regular buns and use spiced apple rings in place of pickles. Finally, forgo the mustard and catsup and top the burgers off with a warm applesauce-mustard sauce.

⅓	cup applesauce
½	teaspoon prepared mustard
2	pita bread rounds
2	spiced apple rings
	Lettuce leaves

● Heat together the applesauce and ½ teaspoon prepared mustard. Cut pita bread rounds and apple rings in half crosswise. To serve, tuck a lettuce leaf, burger half, and apple ring half inside each half of pita bread. Spoon the warmed applesauce-mustard mixture into each. Makes 2 servings.

Santa Fe Stroganoff

1½ pounds beef round steak 2 tablespoons all-purpose flour ½ teaspoon salt 3 tablespoons butter *or* margarine	● Partially freeze meat; thinly slice into bite-size strips. Combine 2 tablespoons flour and the salt; coat meat with the flour mixture. In a large skillet melt butter or margarine. Add meat; brown quickly on both sides.
¾ cup chopped onion 2 to 3 tablespoons rinsed, seeded, and chopped canned jalapeño peppers 2 cloves garlic, minced	● Add chopped onion, chopped jalapeño peppers, and garlic; cook 3 to 4 minutes or till onion is tender.
2 teaspoons instant beef bouillon granules 1 cup hot water ¾ cup dry red wine 2 tablespoons tomato paste ¼ teaspoon ground cumin	● Dissolve bouillon granules in hot water. Stir bouillon mixture, wine, tomato paste, and ground cumin into the meat mixture. Cook, uncovered, over low heat for 1 hour.
1 8-ounce carton dairy sour cream 2 tablespoons all-purpose flour Hot cooked noodles Tomato wedges (optional) Avocado slices (optional)	● Combine the sour cream and 2 tablespoons flour; stir into meat mixture. Cook and stir till thickened and bubbly. Cook and stir 1 minute more. Serve over hot cooked noodles. If desired, garnish with tomato wedges and avocado slices. Makes 6 servings.

It doesn't take a lot of extra know-how or ingredients to make food taste hot and spicy. For example, to make this Mexican version of traditional stroganoff, we simply added a jalapeño or two and a bit of cumin. You'll be amazed at the difference two ingredients can make!

To make the meat easier to slice, freeze it for 1 to 1½ hours.

Sweet-and-Sour Fish

1 **12-ounce package frozen batter-fried fish fillets**	● Prepare fish fillets according to package directions; keep warm.
⅔ **cup chicken broth**	Stir together chicken broth, sugar, vinegar, and soy sauce; stir into cornstarch. Set broth mixture aside.
¼ **cup sugar**	
3 **tablespoons vinegar**	
1½ **teaspoons soy sauce**	
1 **tablespoon cornstarch**	

1 **tablespoon cooking oil**	● Heat a wok or large skillet over high heat; add cooking oil. Stir-fry green pepper pieces, sliced green onions, garlic, ground red pepper, and ground ginger in the hot oil for 3 minutes.
1 **small green pepper, cut into ½-inch pieces**	
3 **green onions, sliced**	
1 **clove garlic, minced**	
½ **teaspoon ground red pepper**	
¼ **teaspoon ground ginger**	

1 **8-ounce can sliced water chestnuts, drained**	● Stir in water chestnuts and mushrooms; stir-fry for 1 minute.
1 **4-ounce can sliced mushrooms, drained**	

Hot cooked rice	● Stir chicken broth mixture; stir into vegetable mixture in wok. Cook and stir till mixture is thickened and bubbly. Cook and stir 2 minutes more. To serve, arrange fish fillets on a bed of rice; spoon vegetable mixture over fish. Serve immediately. Makes 4 servings.

Fix this take-off on an Oriental specialty of the house in the time it takes to bake a package of frozen batter-fried fish fillets.

Besides being sweet and sour, this dish also is slightly hot from the ground red pepper.

Cooking Sausage

Uncooked patties: Thaw patties, if frozen. Place in an unheated skillet. Cook, uncovered, over medium heat for 10 minutes, turning once. Cover and cook 10 minutes more or till thoroughly cooked, turning once. Drain well. (Or, arrange patties on an unheated rack in a shallow baking pan. Bake in a 400° oven for 20 to 25 minutes or till done.)

Uncooked links: Thaw links, if frozen. Do not prick. Place in an unheated skillet. Add ¼ cup cold *water* per *half pound* of sausage. Cover and cook over medium heat for 10 minutes; drain off water. Cook, uncovered, 8 to 10 minutes more or till all liquid has evaporated and sausages are thoroughly cooked, turning occasionally with tongs.

Storing Uncooked Sausage

Wrap uncooked patties, links, or bulk sausage in moisture- and vaporproof wrap; store in refrigerator up to 4 days or freeze up to 2 months before cooking.

Sausage from Scratch

Making your own sausage is easy and fun. Use the instructions on these and the next two pages to make German, Italian, Spanish, or country-style sausage.

Filling Casings

Before making sausage mixture, run cool water through casings; soak in water 2 hours or overnight in refrigerator.

Attach sausage stuffer attachment to electric mixer or food grinder. Using a 3- to 4-foot piece of casing at a time, slip one end and then the remaining length of the casing onto the medium or small stuffer tube.

Using coarse blade of grinder, force sausage mixture through tube till even with tube opening. Pull off two inches of casing and tie a knot. Fill casing firm but not overly full, twisting casing when links are 4 to 5 inches long. If desired, tie with string at twist. Wrap and chill at once.

Breakfast Sausage

Pictured on pages 82 and 83.

6 to 7 feet pork casings (optional) 1 3-pound boneless pork shoulder roast, well chilled	● If making links, see instructions on page 83 for preparing casings. 　Trim fat on chilled pork roast to ¼ inch; discard trimmed fat. Cut meat into ½-inch cubes. With coarse blade of food grinder, grind pork.
1 egg white 1 tablespoon ground sage 2 teaspoons salt 1½ teaspoons black pepper 1 teaspoon ground red pepper ½ teaspoon dried savory, crushed	● In a small bowl beat egg white slightly with a fork. Stir in ground sage, salt, black pepper, ground red pepper, and savory. Add egg white mixture to ground pork; mix thoroughly.
	● Shape sausage into patties, as shown. Or, if desired, fill casings for links. Cook according to instructions on page 82. Makes about 3 pounds.

To shape patties easily, form sausage into 2½-inch-diameter logs. Wrap and freeze. To use, thaw sausage till still icy. Cut *partially* frozen log into ½-inch-thick slices. Thaw completely and cook.

Chorizo

6 to 7 feet pork casings (optional) 1 3-pound boneless pork shoulder roast, well chilled	● If making links, see instructions on page 83 for preparing casings. 　Trim fat from chilled roast. Chop enough fat to make 1 cup; set aside. Discard any remaining fat. 　Cut meat into ½-inch cubes. With coarse blade of food grinder, grind together pork and reserved pork fat.
½ cup white vinegar 3 tablespoons water 3 cloves garlic, minced 2 tablespoons paprika 1 tablespoon chili powder 2½ teaspoons crushed red pepper 2 teaspoons salt 2 teaspoons ground red pepper 1 teaspoon sugar 1 teaspoon black pepper ½ teaspoon coriander seed ½ teaspoon dried oregano, crushed ¼ teaspoon ground cumin	● In a blender container combine vinegar, water, garlic, paprika, chili powder, crushed red pepper, salt, ground red pepper, sugar, black pepper, coriander seed, oregano, and ground cumin; cover and blend till spices are ground. Sprinkle spice mixture evenly over pork; mix thoroughly. 　Shape sausage into patties, as shown above. Or, if desired, fill casings for links. Cook according to instructions on page 82. Makes about 3 pounds.

Chorizo is a hot and peppery Spanish sausage that's well-known in Mexican cooking circles. Because it is often difficult to find outside the Southwestern states, you may want to make your own.

　If you plan to crumble and brown the *Chorizo* for use in another recipe, store it in bulk form rather than shaping it into patties or links.

Italian Sausage

6 to 7 feet pork casings
(optional)
1 3-pound boneless pork
shoulder roast, well
chilled

● If making links, see instructions on page 83 for preparing casings.
Trim fat on chilled roast to ¼ inch; discard trimmed fat. Cut meat into ½-inch cubes. With coarse blade of food grinder, grind pork.

Now you can make your very own blend of Italian sausage. This recipe makes a fairly hot sausage with the distinctive accent of fennel.

2 cloves garlic, minced
1 tablespoon salt
1 tablespoon crushed red
pepper
2 teaspoons ground red
pepper
2 teaspoons paprika
1½ teaspoons fennel seed,
crushed
1 teaspoon dried thyme,
crushed
1 teaspoon coarse ground
black pepper

● In a small bowl thoroughly combine minced garlic, salt, crushed red pepper, ground red pepper, paprika, fennel seed, dried thyme, and coarse ground black pepper. Sprinkle the spice mixture evenly over the ground pork; mix thoroughly till spices are well distributed.

● Shape sausage into patties, as shown on page 84. Or, if desired, fill casings for links. Cook according to instructions on page 82. Makes about 3 pounds.

Bratwurst

6 to 7 feet pork casings

● See instructions on page 83 for preparing casings.

Bratwurst is a German sausage, usually made from pork and veal, that means "frying sausage." Serve with dark, crusty rye bread, spicy German mustard, sauerkraut, and potato salad.

1 2½-pound boneless pork
shoulder roast, well
chilled
½ pound boneless veal, well
chilled

● Trim fat on the chilled pork roast and veal to ¼ inch; discard trimmed fat. Cut meat into ½-inch cubes. With coarse blade of food grinder, grind together pork and veal.

1¾ teaspoons black pepper
1½ teaspoons salt
¾ teaspoon sugar
½ teaspoon dry mustard
½ teaspoon ground mace
½ teaspoon dried marjoram,
crushed
½ teaspoon ground nutmeg

● In a small bowl combine black pepper, salt, sugar, dry mustard, mace, marjoram, and nutmeg. Sprinkle spice mixture evenly over meat; mix thoroughly. With coarse blade of food grinder, grind the meat with the spice mixture till well mixed.

● Fill pork casings using *medium* stuffer. Cook according to instructions on page 82. Makes about 3 pounds.

"Baked" Beans on the Burner

2 slices bacon 1 medium onion, chopped 1 teaspoon chili powder	● In a 2-quart saucepan cook bacon till crisp. Remove bacon, drain, and set aside. Drain fat from pan, reserving *1 tablespoon* drippings in pan. Cook the chopped onion in the reserved drippings till tender but not brown. Add chili powder and cook about 1 minute more.

1 16-ounce can pork and
   beans in tomato sauce
1 4-ounce can diced
   green chili peppers,
   drained
1 tablespoon catsup
1 tablespoon molasses
1 tablespoon prepared
   mustard
¾ teaspoon bottled hot
   pepper sauce
	● Crumble bacon; stir into the onion mixture along with pork and beans, green chili peppers, catsup, molasses, mustard, and hot pepper sauce. Bring to boiling; reduce heat. Simmer, uncovered, about 5 minutes or to desired consistency. Makes 3 servings.

Green chili peppers, chili powder, and hot pepper sauce give these pork and beans a lot of punch. Try this easy side dish with burgers, ribs, or franks.

Creamed Corn with Chilies

1½ teaspoons all-purpose
   flour
1 8-ounce can cream-style
   corn
½ of a 3-ounce package
   cream cheese, cut into
   cubes
	● In a medium saucepan stir the flour into the cream-style corn. Add the cubes of cream cheese. Heat and stir over low heat till the cream cheese is melted.

1 8-ounce can whole
   kernel corn, drained
½ of a 4-ounce can
   (¼ cup) diced green
   chili peppers, drained
¼ cup shredded cheddar,
   Monterey Jack, *or*
   Monterey Jack cheese
   with jalapeño peppers
   (1 ounce)
¼ teaspoon bottled hot
   pepper sauce
⅛ teaspoon onion salt
	● Add whole kernel corn, diced green chili peppers, *half* of the shredded cheese, the hot pepper sauce, and onion salt. Cook and stir over medium heat till the mixture is thickened and bubbly; cook and stir 1 minute more.
	   Transfer the mixture to a serving bowl; sprinkle with the remaining shredded cheese. Makes 3 or 4 servings.

If you don't usually think of creamed corn as spicy and intriguing, our version will change your mind in one bite. Two kinds of cheese, two kinds of corn, and two sources of chili pepper heat make the big difference.

Sesame Broccoli

⅓	**pound broccoli**
2	**teaspoons sesame seed**

● Cut the broccoli lengthwise into spears. Cut crosswise into 2- to 3-inch pieces; set aside.

To toast sesame seed, in a skillet heat sesame seed over low heat about 5 minutes or till golden, stirring often. Remove from skillet; set aside.

2	**tablespoons cooking oil**
1	**small onion, cut into wedges**
2	**cloves garlic, minced**
2	**tablespoons water**

● In the skillet heat oil over medium heat. Add onion, garlic, water, and broccoli. Cover and cook for 7 to 10 minutes or till broccoli is nearly tender.

1	**8-ounce can sliced water chestnuts, drained**
1	**tablespoon soy sauce**
2	**teaspoons dry sherry**
½	**teaspoon ground red pepper**

● Add water chestnuts, soy sauce, sherry, and red pepper. Cook, uncovered, 1 to 2 minutes more or till broccoli is tender, turning broccoli occasionally. Transfer to a serving dish. Sprinkle with toasted sesame seed. Makes 4 servings.

Sesame seed isn't the only spice-shelf ingredient in this side dish. You'll find the mouth-warming sensation from ground red pepper to be persistent, yet pleasant.

Toast the sesame seed in a skillet to bring out its nutty flavor. Then use the same skillet to cook the broccoli.

Potato-Zucchini Curry

¼ cup butter *or* margarine
1 teaspoon dry mustard
1 teaspoon turmeric
¾ teaspoon ground
  coriander
¾ teaspoon ground cumin
½ teaspoon salt
¼ teaspoon ground red
  pepper
	● In a 10-inch skillet heat the butter or margarine till melted. Stir in dry mustard, turmeric, ground coriander, ground cumin, salt, and ground red pepper. Cook and stir the butter-spice mixture over low heat for 5 minutes.

3 large potatoes, peeled and
  cubed (4 cups)
1 large zucchini, sliced *or*
  coarsely shredded
  (2 cups)
1 medium tomato, seeded
  and chopped
	● Stir in potatoes. Cover and cook over medium-low heat for 10 to 15 minutes or till tender, stirring occasionally.
	  Stir in zucchini. Cover and cook about 4 minutes or till tender. Stir in tomato; heat through. Makes 6 to 8 servings.

Curry powder is not one spice but a variable blend of many seasonings. This dish gets its curry color and flavor from turmeric, coriander, cumin, and ground red pepper. Cook the spices together in butter to blend and bring out their flavors.

Louisiana Vegetables and Rice

¼ cup chopped onion
¼ cup chopped green
  pepper
1 clove garlic, minced
1 tablespoon butter *or*
  margarine
	● In a medium saucepan cook onion, green pepper, and garlic in butter or margarine till vegetables are tender.

1 10-ounce can tomatoes
  and green chili peppers
½ of a 10-ounce package
  (1 cup) frozen cut okra,
  thawed
1 cup water
⅓ cup long grain rice
½ teaspoon salt
½ teaspoon ground red
  pepper
¼ teaspoon black pepper
1 bay leaf
	● Stir in tomatoes and green chili peppers, okra, water, rice, salt, red pepper, black pepper, and bay leaf. Bring to boiling; reduce heat. Cover and simmer for 20 to 25 minutes or till rice is tender. Remove bay leaf before serving. Makes 4 servings.

Spice up a whole meal by serving this Southern-style side dish with broiled pork chops, steak, fish, or chicken. The red pepper will heat up your mouth as you eat, but won't overwhelm you or the foods you eat with it.

Zucchini Roma

2 small zucchini
2 green onions

● Slice the zucchini crosswise into ¼- to ½-inch slices. Bias-slice the green onions into ½-inch pieces.

If you like the flavors of good Italian pizza, you'll go for this quick and peppy vegetable dish.

1 tablespoon olive oil *or* cooking oil
1 clove garlic, minced
½ teaspoon dried basil, crushed
½ teaspoon dried oregano, crushed
¼ teaspoon salt
¼ teaspoon dried thyme crushed
¼ teaspoon crushed red pepper

● In a 10-inch skillet heat olive oil or cooking oil. Add the sliced zucchini, bias-sliced green onion, minced garlic clove, dried basil, dried oregano, salt, dried thyme, and crushed red pepper. Cook the vegetables and seasonings in the hot oil for 3 to 4 minutes or till the zucchini is crisp-tender, stirring constantly.

2 small tomatoes, cut into thin wedges

● Add tomato wedges; heat through. Makes 4 servings.

Chili Sauce

Horseradish Sauce
(see recipe, page 92)

Curry Sauce

Chili Sauce

6	medium tomatoes, peeled and chopped
½	cup chopped sweet red pepper *or* green pepper
½	cup chopped onion
1	jalapeño pepper, chopped
1	clove garlic, minced
½	teaspoon dry mustard
¼	teaspoon ground ginger

● In a heavy 3-quart saucepan stir together the peeled and chopped tomatoes, chopped sweet red pepper or green pepper, chopped onion, chopped jalapeño pepper, minced garlic, dry mustard, and ground ginger.

This *Chili Sauce* is similar to, but spicier than, the kind you buy in the supermarket. It has bigger chunks of fresh tomato and sweet peppers, too.

1¼	teaspoons celery seed
¼	teaspoon whole cloves
2	inches stick cinnamon, broken in half

● Tie celery seed, cloves, and cinnamon loosely in several thicknesses of cheesecloth. Add spice bag to tomato mixture. Bring to boiling; reduce heat to medium. Cook, uncovered, for 30 to 40 minutes or till reduced by half.

¾	cup cider vinegar
⅓	cup packed brown sugar
1	teaspoon salt

● Stir in vinegar, brown sugar, and salt. Return to boiling; boil rapidly for 5 minutes, stirring constantly. Remove and discard spice bag. Store sauce in a covered container in refrigerator for up to 2 weeks or freeze. Makes 2¼ cups.

Salsa Cruda

1	large tomato, peeled and finely chopped
2	tablespoons finely chopped onion
1	tablespoon finely chopped green pepper
1	tablespoon finely chopped canned green chili peppers
2	teaspoons finely chopped jalapeño peppers
1	small clove garlic, minced

● In a bowl stir together the peeled and finely chopped tomato, finely chopped onion, finely chopped green pepper, finely chopped canned green chili peppers, finely chopped jalapeño peppers, garlic, and ¼ teaspoon *salt.* Cover; let stand 2 hours to blend flavors. Use as a condiment for meats or tortilla dishes. Serve at room temperature. Makes 1 cup.

Jalapeño peppers make this Mexican table sauce quite peppy. If you like very hot salsa, increase the amount of finely chopped jalapeños to 3 or even 4 teaspoons.

Salsa Cruda   Mustard Mayonnaise

Curry Sauce

| 1 | tablespoon butter *or* margarine |
| 4 | teaspoons curry powder |

● In a saucepan melt the butter or margarine. Add curry powder; cook and stir for 1 to 2 minutes.

1	14½-ounce can chicken broth
½	cup chopped onion
½	cup sliced carrot
1	small tomato, peeled, seeded, and chopped
1	small apple, peeled, cored, and chopped
⅓	cup chopped celery
2	tablespoons coconut
4	teaspoons chutney
1	small clove garlic, minced
1	bay leaf
¼	teaspoon seasoned salt
	Pinch dried thyme, crushed

● Add chicken broth, onion, carrot, tomato, apple, celery, coconut, chutney, garlic, bay leaf, seasoned salt, and thyme. Bring to boiling; reduce heat. Simmer, uncovered, 1 hour or till vegetables are very tender. Remove bay leaf.
  In a blender container or food processor bowl process *half* of the mixture at a time till nearly smooth. Serve warm. Makes about 1⅔ cups.

Fresh vegetables, apple, coconut, and chutney give this sauce its full flavor and appleauce-like texture. Curry powder gives the sauce a mouth-warming spiciness that builds with each bite. Serve it warm with poultry, meat, fish, or cooked vegetables.

Mustard Mayonnaise

3	tablespoons dry mustard
½	teaspoon salt
⅛	teaspoon paprika
	Dash ground red pepper

● In a small mixer bowl combine mustard, salt, paprika, and red pepper.

1	egg yolk
2	tablespoons vinegar
1	cup cooking oil
1	tablespoon lemon juice

● Add egg yolk and vinegar; beat with electric mixer on medium speed till combined. Add oil, 1 teaspoon at a time, beating constantly. Continue beating in oil 1 teaspoon at a time till ¼ cup oil has been added. While continuing to beat, add the remaining oil in a thin, steady stream. Beat in lemon juice. Makes 1⅓ cups.

This creamy dressing has all the qualities of mayonnaise plus the spicy bite of mustard. Use it as a zesty spread on roast beef, turkey, or ham sandwiches. Substitute it for all or part of the mayonnaise in deviled eggs, coleslaw, potato salad, or salad dressings.

Horseradish Sauce

Pictured on page 90.

⅓ cup grated fresh horseradish *or* well-drained prepared horseradish
2 tablespoons mayonnaise *or* salad dressing
1 clove garlic, minced
1 teaspoon dry mustard
1 teaspoon vinegar
½ teaspoon sugar
¼ teaspoon salt
¼ teaspoon black pepper
½ cup whipping cream

● In a bowl stir together horseradish, mayonnaise or salad dressing, garlic, dry mustard, vinegar, sugar, salt, and black pepper till well combined.

In a small mixer bowl whip cream till soft peaks form; fold into the horseradish mixture. Cover and chill at least 1 hour before serving.

Serve with sliced cold meat or poultry. Store in a covered container in the refrigerator up to 2 weeks. Makes 1 cup.

The root of the horseradish plant, named for its resemblance to a horse's hoof, is piercingly pungent. For this recipe, either grate fresh horseradish or use the purchased prepared product. Both will make a fluffy, mildly piquant sauce that enhances cold sliced roast beef, corned beef, pork, and turkey.

Red Pepper Oil

Pictured on page 60.

½ cup sesame oil
⅓ cup crushed red pepper

● In a small saucepan heat sesame oil till warm (200°). Remove from heat. Stir in crushed red pepper. Let stand several hours or overnight. Strain, pressing out oil with a spoon. Store in refrigerator. Makes about ⅓ cup.

Oriental markets call this red-hot concoction "chili oil." Use a tablespoon or two with cooking oil to enliven stir-fries and salad dressings.

Homemade Garam Masala

2 tablespoons whole black peppercorns
4 teaspoons cumin seed
1 tablespoon coriander seed
2 teaspoons whole cloves
1 teaspoon whole cardamom seed (without pods)
3 inches stick cinnamon, broken in half

● To roast spices, place peppercorns, cumin seed, coriander seed, cloves, cardamom seed, and cinnamon in an 8x8x2-inch baking pan. Heat in a 300° oven for 15 minutes.

In a blender container place roasted spices; cover and blend to a fine powder. Store in an airtight container in a cool dry place. Makes about ⅓ cup.

Note: To make Homemade Garam Masala from ground spices, mix 1 tablespoon ground *cumin,* 1 tablespoon ground *coriander,* 2 teaspoons black *pepper,* 2 teaspoons ground *cardamom,* 1 teaspoon ground *cinnamon,* and 1 teaspoon ground *cloves.* Makes ¼ cup.

Garam Masala is an essential seasoning in the cuisine of Northern India. The aromatic spices in this variable blend are those that the Indians say heat the body. Add it sparingly, usually toward the end of cooking.

Though grinding your own garam masala gives the freshest flavor, you also can purchase it at Asian markets or mix spices that are already ground (see recipe note).

Homemade Chili Powder

4 dried hot chili peppers
3 dried ancho peppers

● See instructions on page 6 for handling chili peppers. Remove stems and seeds. Cut peppers into small pieces.

4 teaspoons cumin seed
1 teaspoon garlic powder
1 teaspoon ground coriander
1 teaspoon dried oregano
½ teaspoon whole cloves

● In a blender container combine cut-up peppers, cumin seed, garlic powder, ground coriander, oregano, and whole cloves. Cover and grind to a fine powder. Store in an airtight container in a cool dry place. Makes about ⅓ cup.

Once you discover the fresh, pronounced flavor of *Homemade Chili Powder,* you may decide to make it a pantry-shelf staple.
For dried hot chili peppers, use pequin, cayenne, or the whole red chili peppers from the grocer's spice section.

Homemade Five-Spice Powder

1 teaspoon ground cinnamon
1 teaspoon crushed aniseed *or* 1 star anise, crushed
¼ teaspoon crushed fennel seed
¼ teaspoon freshly ground black pepper *or* Szechuan pepper
⅛ teaspoon ground cloves

● In a bowl stir together ground cinnamon, crushed aniseed or star anise, crushed fennel seed, ground black pepper or Szechuan pepper, and ground cloves. Store the spice mixture in an airtight container in a cool dry place. Makes about 1 tablespoon.

Many supermarkets carry this Oriental seasoning, but you may have the spices on hand to make your own. If you crave the truly authentic, look for star anise and Szechuan pepper at any Oriental food market.

Homemade Curry Powder

4½ teaspoons ground coriander
2 teaspoons turmeric
1¼ teaspoons cumin seed
½ to 1 teaspoon whole black peppercorns
½ to 1 teaspoon crushed red pepper
½ teaspoon whole cardamom seed (without pods)
½ inch stick cinnamon
¼ teaspoon whole cloves
¼ teaspoon ground ginger

● In a blender container place ground coriander, turmeric, cumin seed, whole black peppercorns, crushed red pepper, whole cardamom seed, stick cinnamon, whole cloves, and ground ginger; cover and grind for 1 to 2 minutes or till mixture is a fine powder.
Store spice mixture in an airtight container in a cool dry place. Makes about ¼ cup.

Curry powder is really a shortcut to the highly esteemed flavors of Indian cuisine. No two blends are alike and there can be as many as 20 different spices in a blend. Expect more intense flavor from freshly made curry powder than from commercial blends.
To get the most well-rounded flavor, cook curry powder in a little butter or oil at the beginning of a recipe.

Index

Tips